Novena

Novena

THE POWER OF PRAYER

Barbara Calamari & Sandra DiPasqua

PENGUIN
STUDIO

PENGUIN STUDIO
Published by the Penguin Group
Penguin Putnam Inc., 375 Hudson Street,
New York, New York 10014, U.S.A.
Penguin Books Ltd, 27 Wrights Lane,
London W8 5TZ, England
Penguin Books Australia Ltd, Ringwood,
Victoria, Australia
Penguin Books Canada Ltd, 10 Alcorn Avenue,
Toronto, Ontario, Canada M4V 3B2
Penguin Books (N.Z.) Ltd, 182-190 Wairau Road,
Auckland 10, New Zealand

Penguin Books Ltd, Registered Offices:
Harmondsworth, Middlesex, England

First published in 1999 by Penguin Studio,
a member of Penguin Putnam Inc.

1 3 5 7 9 10 8 6 4 2

Images reproduced with permission of
peka Verlags-GmbH, D-82234 Wessling, Germany.

CIP data avalible

ISBN 0-670-88444-8

Printed in Japan
Set in Adobe Garamond
Designed by Sandra DiPasqua

Preface

THIS BOOK IS THE RESULT OF OUR DESIRE TO EXPLORE and celebrate what has been to us a mysterious yet profoundly meaningful ritual: the recitation of novenas. In many Catholic churches throughout the world, you will find folded pieces of paper with prayers, often addressed to a particular saint, written on them. These written devotions, left behind in gratitude, attest to answered prayers, offering hope to others in distress. We created *Novena* as a compilation of these folded paper prayers. Believing strongly in prayer, we wanted to present the beauty and the power of the novena. The prayers you find here were gathered from many different sources—church benches, prayer cards, Catholic pamphlets, prayer books as well as the Internet.

We also wanted to celebrate the tradition of praying to a particular saint or angel, or to the madonna and the imagery associated with these figures. Raised surrounded by the images on old devotional cards, specially painted in honor of each novena, we wanted to include them in this book. Many looking at them will experience the shock of instant recognition. As familiar to us as old family photographs, the images on these cards were displayed in the homes of relatives and friends throughout our childhoods. Though some may seem gory and bizarre, they exude a dreamy mystery and religious symbolism that seem lacking in our modern-day culture.

The visual style of this book was developed in order to present the novena in a new light while also reminding us of its tradition. It was our intention to create a book that would be accessible to all, Catholic and non-Catholic alike. Both of us remember people who led totally secular, even sophisticated, lives, who never set foot in a church for Sunday mass yet who would constantly appeal to their patron saint for favors or bring lilies to Saint Anthony of Padua on his birthday. These people prayed because the novena really works, regardless of which religious tradition one embraces.

Though certainly not experts on this subject, we have tried to answer the main questions that we ourselves have asked about this devotion: Why is everything in nines? Why are certain saints invoked for particular favors? Why are there so many different prayers directed to the madonna? We have included a short biographical sketch of each saint's life, which, we hope, provides some illumination as to why he or she became the patron saint of particular subjects, locations, occupations, and causes. We have also included a topic index of the problems and patronages handled by each saint, which is, in turn, cross-referenced to his or her location in the book.

We are thankful to Mr. Fred L. Pfefferlein of Peka Verlag in Germany. The Peka devotional cards are the images in this book. Commonly distributed as holy cards, they are the visual equivalent of the novena. Karen Dottling has been an indispensable research assistant and we would like to acknowledge her expertise and willingness to help, often at a moment's notice. We would also like to thank our agent, Mary South, and our editor, Marie Timell, of Penguin Studio for taking the leap of faith that got this project off the ground. Finally, it is said that of all the saints it is Saint Anthony of Padua and Saint Jude who seem to inspire the deepest devotion. This book is created in thanks to both of them for our own answered prayers.

—Barbara Calamari and Sandra DiPasqua

the novenas

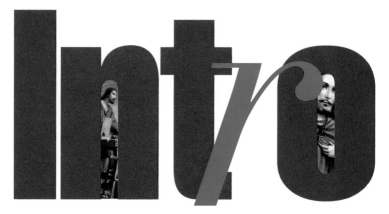

THE POWER OF PRAYER

PRAYER, AFFIRMATION, DECLARATION, AND INTENTION.
More and more people are opening themselves to forms of devotion such as these. All represent the desire or will for a specific result or change. Although the power of prayer may be fully understood only by those who experience it, the purpose of prayer is to open a channel to the divine and, in faith, to give our troubles to God.

A novena is a prayer repeated to obtain a requested intention or spiritual grace. Frequently said when one is in a desperate or hopeless state, when all else fails, recitation of a novena and adherence to its rules of repetition can be the act of sacrifice necessary to invoke a power greater than our own. It can express one's willingness to accept divine intervention in the solution of a problem. The repetition of the prayer helps to gradually clear the mind of all distraction in order to put its focus on the requested intention. Not only is it a spiritual sacrifice, but it is also a way to allow the subconscious to face a real problem and to consider solutions for it.

The word "novena" comes from the Latin word *novem,* or nine; that is, novenas are usually based in some way on the number nine. Most novenas are said nine times in a row for nine days in a row. If ten is the mystical number of God and perfection, then nine is the number nearest perfection, though not perfect. Both the Pythagoreans and early Christian monks considered nine to be the number of humanity. The tradition of setting nine days aside for prayers predates Christianity. Both the Greeks and Romans dedicated nine days after a death to prayers of mourning for the deceased. On the ninth day a special feast was held, completing the funeral rites. The Romans also had yearly novenas dedicated to departed relatives.

Catholics consider the very first novena to have been created by Jesus Christ himself. Before Christ rose into heaven he instructed his apostles to spend nine days praying for divine guidance as they awaited the arrival of the Holy Spirit. After the apostles spent this allotted time in prayer, the Holy Spirit appeared to them in the form of tongues of fire coming from the sky. These tongues rested on each apostle, giving them the gift of many languages and the burning desire to spread the story of Jesus Christ. It is thought that the nine-day tradition of prayer comes from this first novena. The novena of the Holy Spirit was written in the Middle Ages to commemorate this event, and so it is presented as the last and most important novena in this book (page 148).

Invoking the saints for help in healing illnesses and stopping plagues became very common by the first millennium. As the cult of saints grew from early times to the Middle Ages, their legends and relics became more revered. Because it was thought that these people lived the most Christ-like lives, they were honored for their sanctity and their bodies were considered more than human, inviolable by death and invested with divine healing powers. That is why the bodies of many of these early saints were cut up and distributed to churches in various locations to be venerated and used in blessings. It was thought to be a physical way for the average person to share in the divine presence. In seventeenth-century Spain the Christmas novena was instituted. For nine days preceding Christmas Day, each symbolizing a month the infant Jesus spent in the womb, a special novena was said. Many towns in France and southern Italy began doing nine-day novenas in preparation for their local saint's feast day. It became customary to invoke the saint for a requested favor that would be granted in this time of celebration. Fearing that novenas would be used in superstition, the Church began to recognize them only in the mid-1800s. Of the many novenas, only thirty-two are officially recommended, mainly in honor of a feast day. Personal novenas for individualized intentions continue to be a very private form of prayer.

Most of the novenas in this book are addressed to a particular saint and request that he or she intercede with God on our behalf. Many of our immediate problems, being material in nature, are thought to be best understood by saints who have endured a human existence. While it should never seem foolish and frivolous to ask God for help in dealing with an unfaithful spouse or credit-card debt, the saints, having been human, might have made similar errors in judgment themselves. Not only do they understand our problems, but they are also devoted to guiding us on a clearer path, committed in life and in death to raising our spiritual level. They help us realize that God is intimately involved in our daily lives.

The saints all have differing fields of expertise based on the earthly lives they led. Novenas are said to certain saints to help us deal with problems similar to those they suffered. Saint Rita of Cascia had a terrible marriage and is invoked for marital stability; Saint Peregrine suffered with cancer and is invoked for a cure; Saint Joseph had the responsibility of protecting and supporting the Holy Family and so he is invoked to find work. The mystical essence of the saints is also part of their attraction. Some represent an attribute, such as fierce devotion, Saint Agnes or Saint Jude, for example. Others offer a sweet welcome, such as Saint Anthony of Padua or Saint Theresa of Lisieux.

There are at least eleven official novenas to the Virgin Mary, and we have included six of them in our collection. In all of those included she takes on the role of the universal mother. She can be frightening and severe, as she is in Fatima; the most loving and open of mothers, as she is at Guadalupe; or she can be the refuge of God himself, as she is in Our Lady of Perpetual Help. Considered the most perfect example of the human race ever born, Mary is exalted above all saints and angels.

The novenas compiled in this book can be used as a jumping-off point, to start a dialogue, and do not have to be strictly adhered to. The topic index (page 155) contains a general listing of subjects and which saints to invoke for health, emotional, or material problems. The most popular novena saints are Saint Anthony of Padua, Saint Rita of Cascia, and Saint Jude. If you have never done a novena before, it is best to familiarize yourself with the images and stories accompanying the prayers. Any saint or angel who feels familiar and sympathetic to you can be asked to intercede for anything. Generally, the saints are invoked for more material or health-related problems while the angels are invoked for more universal problems or to change a life path. The madonna can be invoked for anything but is most effective for those in distress of the soul, the guilt-ridden, and those troubled by family discord. The novenas directed toward God himself are the most spiritual and intense. Bear in mind that the only prayer that can be guaranteed to be answered is "Thy Will Be Done." In praying we participate in God's unfolding will for the world and ourselves.

The repetition of the prayer nine times for nine days seems like a simple formula but it can be more difficult to keep than one thinks. The novena should not be looked upon with superstition. If one skips a day of prayer it does not mean that the problem will not be solved or that the other days in prayer have been nullified. The novena can be used merely to develop a habit of addressing a higher power. Novenas are said to be the most honoring of a saint when said nine days before a particular saint's feast day, the last day of the novena coinciding with the saint's feast day. While praying to a saint, invoke him or her with all your heart. The saints are there to help you.

Why do novenas work? Is it the willingness to open to the miraculous? Or is it simply setting aside time to address a problem that is crucial? Perhaps by repeating a request for a solution over and over, we are taking the fear out of a problem. Or is it that we open to grace? Prayer brings grace, and grace lightens the spirit and makes the day go easier. The more grace infuses us and the less the material world seems to bother us, the closer we are to our pure essence in spirit. Novenas are not magic. They are just another form of prayer. Yet the discipline required in this form of devotion assures us of spending time with a higher level of being, bringing divine blessing and grace into the world.

the Sa

St. Thomas Aquinas

1225–1274

CONSIDERED MORE ANGELIC THAN HUMAN, Saint Thomas Aquinas has the title of "Angelic Doctor." His life is the story of someone who lived totally through his higher mind, rejecting all worldly temptations, ambitions, and pleasures in favor of intellectual pursuit. Honored in his own lifetime, he was continually invited by the Pope and the king of France to share his learning, but this never changed his kind disposition or the simple way he lived his life. He refused all offers of holy office in order to continue his vocation of studying, writing, and preaching. Because of this love of learning for its own sake, Saint Thomas Aquinas is the patron saint of students. He is invoked whenever there is a difficult situation regarding education, be it tackling a difficult subject or passing an entrance examination. Although this novena is written for his patronage of Catholic schools, all students should feel free to call on him.

Saint Thomas Aquinas is regarded by most historians as the greatest thinker and theologian of the Middle Ages. Yet the more knowledge he mastered, the more he realized how much he did not know. Born at Roccasecca, near Naples, he was the youngest child of the count of Aquino. At the age of five he was sent away to the Benedictines of Monte Cassino. There, at that young age, he displayed great intellectual acuity and easily surpassed all the other students in his class. His father, being a nobleman, assumed that he would be trained for a high ecclesiastical office. At the age of seventeen, Saint Thomas scandalized his

S. THOMAS AQUINAS

Not only were you a great teacher, you lived a life of virtue and you made holiness the desire of your heart. If I cannot imitate you in the brilliance of your academic pursuits, I can follow you in the humility and charity that marked your life.

family when they discovered that he had secretly joined the new order of Dominican friars. This order frequently resorted to begging in the streets to survive. His brothers then kidnapped him and locked him in the family house for the next year. Trying to get him to break his vows, they presented him with every temptation, including a beautiful prostitute. Saint Thomas chased her away with a flaming torch and from that day was freed of any sexual desires. His family finally relented and released him. In 1248 he went to the city of Cologne, where he studied under Saint Albert the Great, at that time the most brilliant professor in Europe. His lumbering presence and slow movements belied his genius, causing his fellow students to refer to Saint Thomas as "the Dumb Ox." He began publishing his works at the age of twenty-two and then went on to Paris, where he earned his doctorate in theology. He was in great demand as a university professor and became famous for his lucid writings. The great challenge of his life was to explain Christianity in Aristotelian terms.

In 1266 Saint Thomas Aquinas began his greatest work, *Summa Theologica.* Seven years and two million words later, he quite suddenly stopped work on it, leaving it unfinished. While attending mass he had had an ecstatic vision, and afterward he declared that compared with what he had just seen, "all that writing seemed like so much straw." He died three months later, at the age of forty-nine. So simple, pure, and ingenuous had Saint Thomas Aquinas remained in his life that his deathbed confessor declared his final confession to be akin to that of a five-year-old child.

His feast day is January 28.

the
NOVENA

Saint Thomas Aquinas, patron of students and schools, I thank God for the gifts of light and knowledge God bestowed on you, which you used to build up the church in love. I thank God, too, for the wealth and richness of theological teaching you left in your writings. Not only were you a great teacher, you lived a life of virtue and you made holiness the desire of your heart. If I cannot imitate you in the brilliance of your academic pursuits, I can follow you in the humility and charity that marked your life. As Saint Paul said, charity is the greatest gift, and is open to all. Pray for me that I may grow in holiness and charity. Pray also for Catholic schools and for all students. In particular, please obtain the favor I ask during this novena. Amen.

(Mention your request.)

**Say this novena nine times in a row
for nine days in a row.**

St. Agatha

Third Century

SO FIERCE ARE THE POWERS ATTRIBUTED
to Saint Agatha, it is said that even pagans and Jews flocked
to pay homage to her soon after her death. Martyred in
A.D. 251, Saint Agatha is credited with keeping the fires of
Mount Etna from erupting and engulfing her home city of
Catania in Italy. Millions of people still parade in her
honor on her feast day. God's reaction to her martyrdom
was great and instantaneous: as she was being tortured a
major earthquake erupted. Her crypt bears the inscription
"Do not offend Agatha's nation, because she will avenge all
offenses."

Saint Agatha was a great beauty of noble birth. Raised a
Christian, her parents died and left her well endowed in
both property and money. Quintianus, the Roman consul
in Sicily, felt she would make him a perfect wife. Using the
recent ruling of the Roman emperor against the Christian
religion as a pretense, he had Agatha brought before him
and proposed marriage. She refused the proposal, explaining that she had dedicated her virginity to Christ. When
she refused to renounce her religion, he became enraged
and had her taken to a brothel run by a woman named
Aphrodosia and her nine daughters. There Agatha was
forced to live as a prostitute for thirty days. This was a
common punishment at that time for Christian virgins.
Agatha was so miserable there, weeping to be martyred,
that Aphrodosia returned her to Quintianus, saying, "It
would be easier to split rocks or reduce iron to the softness
of lead than to move or recall that girl's mind from its

*Protect us against rape and other
violations, guard us against breast cancer
and other afflictions of women, and
inspire us to overcome adversity.*

Christian intention." After Agatha again refused to for-
swear her religion, Quintianus had her stretched on a rack
and tortured. Suffering her torments almost cheerfully,
Agatha continually invoked Christ as her savior. Quintianus then had her breasts slowly crushed and cut off. She
was sent back to prison, without food, water, or medical
attention. In the middle of the night, Saint Peter appeared
to Agatha and cured all her wounds, restoring her breasts.
Four days later, she was again brought before Quintianus,
who was unimpressed with her miraculous healing. She
was stripped naked and rolled in burning coals and broken
pieces of pottery. Just as this was occurring, a massive
earthquake erupted, destroying Catania. The people of the
city ran in, yelling that this was happening because of the
unjust treatment of Agatha. While Quintianus fruitlessly
attempted to escape, Agatha begged to join Christ in
heaven and she died.

Incredible miracles and healings began to occur immediately following her death and entombment. A year after
her burial, as Mount Etna erupted and its lava flow threat-
ened the city, Saint Agatha's death shroud was raised in
supplication and the lava flow miraculously stopped. The
result was that the majority of the pagans living in the region converted to Christianity. Because of her mutilation
and healing, Saint Agatha is the patroness of breast disease.
She is depicted with the palms of martyrdom; sometimes
she is carrying her breasts on a dish. Interestingly, she is
also the patroness of bell founders, either because bells resemble breasts in shape or because they are used as fire
alarms. She is also invoked against volcanic eruptions.

Her feast day is February 5.

the NOVENA

O Saint Agatha, who withstood the unwelcome advances from unwanted suitors, and suffered pain and torture for your devotion to our Lord, we celebrate your faith, dignity, and martyrdom.

Protect us against rape and other violations, guard us against breast cancer and other afflictions of women, and inspire us to overcome adversity.

O Saint Agatha, virgin and martyr, mercifully grant that we who venerate your sacrifice may receive your intercession. Amen.

(Mention your request.)

**Say this novena nine times in a row
for nine days in a row.**

St. Patrick

389–461

THOUGH NOT USUALLY CONSIDERED A novena saint, Saint Patrick is called upon by many for faith in the most trying of circumstances. Since he himself was forced to submit to living in a country not of his own choosing, he assists in accepting difficult situations where there is little hope of change. The patron saint of Ireland, he is credited with single-handedly changing the beliefs of the entire Irish nation through the purity and intensity of his faith. Saint Patrick's following has spread to wherever the Irish have settled, especially in North America and Australia. He could never have imagined the astounding impact that his work in Ireland would have on the world.

Saint Patrick was born on the west coast of Great Britain of Roman-British parents. Though his father was a deacon and his grandfather a priest, early on, Patrick showed no interest at all in God or religion. At the age of sixteen he was abducted by pirates and taken to Ireland, where he was sold into slavery. For six years he was forced to live under the direst of conditions, subject to the elements and hardship, herding sheep. When he began to pray for deliverance, he dreamed of a ship docked two hundred miles away. By following the dream's directions, he was able to escape from captivity, find the ship, and prevail upon the sailors to take him with them. He eventually returned to his family, and in gratitude for God's help he became a priest. In A.D. 432 he again had a dream that changed the course of his life. In it, he was instructed to return to Ireland and to convert as many people as possible to Chris-

Ask for all who dwell in this land and the land of thy labors the precious light of faith, and beg for us on whom its glorious rays have long since beamed, the grace to regulate our lives by its sacred maxims.

tianity. Though he would have preferred to perfect his studies and remain in Britain, he surrendered to the guidance of the dream and put all his faith in God by returning to Ireland. Living there at a time when the Druid religion was in decline, he nonetheless had to compete with the "wizardry" of the Druid priests. There are many fantastic tales of his magical powers. It was said that Saint Patrick could turn people into deer and that he could turn day into night. He is still invoked today by those afraid of snakes, because he was said to have obtained a promise from God that no poisonous reptiles would be allowed to live on that island. Saint Patrick expelling snakes is a common image. Another one of his symbols is the shamrock, or three-leaf clover. This symbolizes how he explained the Holy Trinity in his preaching.

Saint Patrick built his main church in Northern Ireland. Realizing that the landowners chose the religion of their serfs for them, he set upon converting the major families first. His life as a former slave and fugitive taught him to trust God completely, and those living in similarly miserable circumstances have always been able to easily identify with him. He died in 461 in the monastery of Saul, and his remains are buried with those of Saint Brigid in Ulster.

HIS FEAST DAY IS MARCH 17.

the NOVENA

O great apostle of Ireland, glorious Saint Patrick, to whom under God so many are indebted for the most precious of all treasures, the great gift of faith, receive our fervent thanks for the zeal and charity that have been to thousands the source of blessings so invaluable. We ask your intervention in receiving (mention your request). Ask for all who dwell in this land and the land of thy labors the precious light of Faith, and beg for us on whom its glorious rays have long since beamed, the grace to regulate our lives by its sacred maxims. Amen.

**Say this novena nine times in a row
for nine days in a row.**

St. JOSEPH

A POOR CARPENTER AND A DIRECT DESCEN-
dant of the house of David, Saint Joseph was selected by
God from all the men in the world to be the earthly father
of Jesus Christ, an average person exalted to the highest
level of respect and achievement. He readily accepted this
and other directives from God and never shirked his responsibility to his family. Thus Joseph epitomizes the role
of father-protector. Many of the greatest saints have called
on Joseph for protection. His novena is considered to be
powerful, one that can be invoked for any trouble. Saint
Teresa of Avila said, "I don't recall up to this day ever having petitioned him for anything that he fails to grant. It is
an amazing thing, the great many favors God has granted
me through the mediation of this blessed saint." In Italy,
where his feast day is a major religious holiday, Saint
Joseph is believed to have the power to break all natural
laws. It is said that since Jesus always obeyed Joseph when
he was his father on earth, Joseph is accorded the same
power in heaven.

The only information known about Joseph is written in
the Gospels. Because of the chasteness of his marriage to
Mary, it is often assumed that he was an older man. This is
unlikely considering the amount of effort he exerted protecting the Holy Family. Joseph was betrothed to Mary
when he learned of her pregnancy. He was prevented from
leaving her when he was assured by an angel in a dream
that Mary was still a virgin and the child that she was carrying was divinely given. After the child Jesus was born in

To you we raise our hearts and hands to ask your powerful intercession in obtaining from the compassionate heart of Jesus all the helps and graces necessary for our spiritual and temporal welfare.

Bethlehem, Joseph was again visited by the angelic presence, instructing him to move his family into Egypt to avoid King Herod's slaughter of the innocents. He kept his family in Egypt until the death of Herod seven years later. He then moved Jesus and Mary back to Israel, settling in the obscure town of Nazareth in Galilee. Joseph approached the responsibility of raising the son of God with great humility and simplicity, instructing the boy in the trade of carpenter. He accepted and protected his wife's virginity and led a chaste life devoted to his faith in God. In art he usually is shown holding a lily for purity. In some images he is carrying the baby Jesus. The last mention of Joseph in the Gospels is when Jesus was twelve years old and left his parents to preach in the temple. It is assumed that Joseph died before the wedding feast of Cana. Since he enjoyed a perfect family life with Jesus and Mary, it is also assumed that Joseph died an easy death, with his wife and son at his side. This is why one of Saint Joseph's many patronages is for a happy death.

Because of his livelihood as a carpenter, he is considered the patron of workers. He is frequently invoked by those in need of work. In the United States people bury a statue of him upside down on the properties of hard-to-sell homes.

HIS PATRONAGES INCLUDE A HAPPY DEATH
AND THE COUNTRIES OF BELGIUM, CANADA,
AND PERU. HIS FEAST DAY IS MARCH 19.

the
NOVENA

O glorious Saint Joseph, faithful follower of Jesus Christ, to you we raise our hearts and hands to ask your powerful intercession in obtaining from the compassionate heart of Jesus all the helps and graces necessary for our spiritual and temporal welfare, particularly the grace of a happy death, and the special grace for which we now ask.

(Mention your request.)

O guardian of the Word Incarnate, we feel animated with confidence that your prayers for us will be graciously heard at the throne of God.

(The following is to be said seven times in honor of the seven joys and seven sorrows of Saint Joseph:)

O glorious Saint Joseph, through the love you bear for Jesus Christ, and for the glory of his name, hear our prayers and grant our petitions.

This novena can be practiced at any time of year. It is particularly effective if done for the seven Sundays prior to the feast of Saint Joseph in honor of his seven sorrows and seven joys. **Say this novena nine times in a row for nine days in a row.**

St. Catherine of Siena

1347–1380

ACTION AND ACTIVISM ARE THE ESSENCE of Saint Catherine of Siena. Passionately devoted to the salvation of mankind, she left an astounding legacy of four hundred written letters and a devotional *Dialogue* that are considered great classics in literature. She is credited with influencing the return of the papacy to Rome from Avignon, and for this reason she is the patroness of Italy. Known for her incredible charm, she horrified her wealthy parents by her willingness to express her devotion to Christ through corporal humiliations and long periods of fasting. Counselor and advisor to those in power, it was said that she perfected the art of kissing the Pope's feet while simultaneously twisting his arm. Saint Catherine struggled against great odds to keep the Catholic Church united. Her novena is a call for faith in troubled times. She is invoked to engender the strength and faith for action in times when action is needed, both political and spiritual.

Born Caterina Benincasa, the youngest of twenty-five children, Saint Catherine's father was a wealthy dyer. At the age of six she had a mystical vision of Christ surrounded by saints. A beautiful and cheerful child, she alarmed her parents by spending much of her time in prayer and meditation. She grew devoted to Christ and, like him, wanted to take on the suffering of the entire world, secretly mortifying her flesh and fasting for days. Saint Catherine is the patroness of fire protection because her sister saw her deep in prayer in the kitchen, engulfed in flames from the stove. When she was pulled out, there was

S.TA CATHARINA

Help us to pass unscathed through the
corruption of this world, and to remain
unshakably faithful to the church in
word, deed, and example.

no evidence of burn marks on her body. Her parents, wanting a normal daughter, were angry at her refusal to marry or to improve her personal appearance. They finally gave in to her religious cravings and allowed her to become a tertiary (lay person) in the Order of Saint Dominic. She lived at home and went out to work, caring for those with the most repulsive diseases when no one else would help them. For this reason, Saint Catherine is also known as the patron saint of nursing services. Because of her great spiritual insight and radiantly happy outlook, she attracted a following in Siena known as the Caterinati. They did much to revitalize an interest in spirituality in Siena and its surrounding regions. On the Fourth Sunday of Lent in 1375, Saint Catherine received the stigmata: the wounds of Christ appeared on her body and then disappeared, visible only to her.

Illiterate, Saint Catherine dictated hundreds of letters and spiritual writings to her secretaries. It was her constant barrage of letters to Pope Gregory XI that influenced him to move the papacy back from Avignon to Rome. She later became the adviser to his successor, the arrogant and difficult Urban VI. When he caused a great schism in the church, the College of Cardinals having voted in a rival Pope to return to Avignon, Saint Catherine remained loyal to Urban. She lectured him in countless letters on how best to improve himself. At his invitation, she moved to Rome to work as a papal adviser. When she died there of a stroke at the age of thirty-three, the wounds of the stigmata reappeared on her body.

Her feast day is April 29.

the
NOVENA

Heavenly Father, your glory is in your saints. We praise your glory in the life of the admirable Saint Catherine of Siena, virgin and doctor of the church. Her whole life was a noble sacrifice inspired by an ardent love of Jesus, your unblemished lamb. In troubled times she strenuously upheld the rights of his beloved spouse, the church. Father, honor her merits and hear her prayers for each of us, and for our whole parish family dedicated to her. Help us to pass unscathed through the corruption of this world, and to remain unshakably faithful to the church in word, deed, and example. Help us always to see in the Vicar of Christ an anchor in the storms of life and a beacon of light to the harbor of your love, in this dark night of your times and men's souls. Grant also to each of us our special petition. We ask this through Jesus, your Son, in the bond of the Holy Spirit. Amen.

(Pause to pray for your own intentions.)

Saint Catherine of Siena, pray for us.

**Say this novena nine times in a row
for nine days in a row.**

St. Peregrine

1265–1345

SAINT PEREGRINE EXPERIENCED FIRSTHAND the despair of the incurably ill. Stricken with a gangrenous cancer, he came to accept not only the severity of his illness, but also the miracle of his healing at the hands of Christ. As a result of Saint Peregrine's example of acceptance and faith, he has many followers the world over, particularly among those who are seriously ill. He is invoked for medical breakthroughs, for those stricken with serious ailments, and for protection against diseases. He is the patron of those suffering from cancer, running sores, or any incurable disease.

Saint Peregrine was an unlikely candidate for sainthood. Born into a wealthy family in Forli, Italy, Peregrine was a leader in that town's antipapal political party. When the Pope sent Philip Benizi the prior general of the Servants of Mary, to Forli to attempt reconciliation with the party, he was violently attacked. Peregrine himself hit Philip in the face. The effect of this forever changed his life. Instead of retaliating or running away, Philip turned the other cheek and gazed at Peregrine in loving forgiveness. Peregrine collapsed in shame and begged to be forgiven. Philip recommended that he transform his life by cultivating a childlike devotion to the Mother of God. Peregrine converted to Catholicism and proceeded to spend much of his time praying in the cathedral at Forli. In a vision, he was directed by the Virgin Mary to go to Siena and join the religious order of the Servants of Mary. On becoming a priest, Peregrine returned to the town of Forli and, there, dedi-

St. PEREGRINE, O.S.M.

For so many years you bore in your own flesh this cancerous disease that destroys the very fiber of our being, and you had recourse to the source of all grace when the power of man could do no more.

cated himself to working with the sick, the poor, and the people on the fringes of society. It was reported that many miracle healings and cures occurred as the result of his inspiring masses. In his devotion, Saint Peregrine imposed upon himself the penance of never sitting down and slept only on the cold ground, using a stone for a pillow. He continued the practice for thirty years. This resulted in severe varicose veins which eventually led to an open, running sore on his leg, diagnosed as cancer. At the age of sixty he found himself in the same situation as those he had been serving. The putrid smell of his wound caused him to be ostracized by his associates and society in general. A surgeon recommended immediate amputation. On the eve of the operation, Saint Peregrine crept into the chapel and prayed, falling into a trancelike sleep in which he saw Christ get off the crucifix, bend over him, and touch his leg. When Peregrine awoke, his leg was completely healed. Word of this miracle spread rapidly and many stricken with incurable illnesses flocked to Forli for his prayers.

Saint Peregrine lived as a healer for another twenty years and died at the age of eighty in Forli. He was canonized nearly four hundred years later, in 1726. At that time his tomb was reopened and the air was filled with the smell of flowers. It was discovered that his body had never decomposed. His tomb continues to be a site of miraculous healings, and there are many shrines and healing societies bearing his name.

Saint Peregrine is particularly popular in Spain and Austria. His feast day is May 2.

the NOVENA

O great Saint Peregrine, you who have been called "the Mighty" and "the Wonder Worker" because of the numerous miracles you have had recourse to, for so many years you bore in your own flesh this cancerous disease that destroys the very fiber of our being, and you had recourse to the source of all grace when the power of man could do no more. You were favored with the vision of Jesus coming down from his Cross to heal your affliction. Ask of God and our Lady the cure of these sick persons whom we entrust to you. Aided in this way by your powerful intercession, we shall sing to God, now and for all eternity, a song of gratitude for his great goodness and mercy.

(Mention your request.)

Saint Peregrine, pray for me and for all who invoke your aid. Amen.

Say this novena nine times in a row for nine days in a row.

St. Dymphra

605–620

BECAUSE OF HER PERSONAL KNOWLEDGE of the terror and misery caused by madness, Saint Dymphna offers great comfort and consolation to those afflicted with mental disorders and also to their families. Her burial site continues to be a place of miraculous healing, and Gheel, in Belgium, the town where it is located, leads the world as a center for the treatment of the mentally ill. Saint Dymphna lived for such a short time, so long ago, there is little to prove that she ever really existed.

Saint Dymphna was born in Ireland. Her father, Damon, was a pagan king, and her mother was a Christian. Dymphna was raised in her mother's faith and was very devout. When Dymphna was fourteen, her mother died, and her father became so engulfed in grief that he sank into mental illness. He sent messengers throughout the land to find a woman of noble birth who resembled his wife, so he might marry her. None could be found. Dymphna, however, so resembled his dead wife that he decided to marry her even though she was his daughter. In order to avoid this fate, Dymphna fled from the castle with her confessor, Saint Gerebran. They traveled abroad, first to Antwerp, then finally settling in Gheel. Within a year her father found them living as hermits. He had the priest beheaded and begged Dymphna to return home with him. When she refused, he drew his sword and chopped off her head. Both bodies were buried immediately. She was fifteen years old at the time of her death. In those days, epileptics and the mentally ill were treated as pariahs and left to

*O God, we humbly beseech you through
your servant, Saint Dymphna, who
sealed with blood the love she bore you,
to grant relief to those who suffer from
mental afflictions and nervous disorders.*

roam. Shortly after Saint Dymphna's death, five such sufferers went to sleep at the site where she was killed and were instantly healed by the blood in the earth.

The legend of Saint Dymphna became very popular in the early thirteenth century when the bodily remains of an unknown man and woman were dug up and the name Dymphna was written on a brick found on the coffin of the woman. As the remains were reinterred in a tomb, miraculous healings of those suffering from epilepsy and mental illness were reported in the immediate area. The bishop of Cambrai commissioned a text of the life of Saint Dymphna which drew on oral reports for its information. The tomb became a pilgrimage site for those suffering from mental afflictions. By the end of the thirteenth century a hospital was built near Dymphna's tomb for the treatment of nervous and mental illnesses. Today, Gheel remains a world-renowned hospital center, offering the most enlightened methods in treating the mentally ill, and the residents of that city are known for their kindness toward those so afflicted. As many as two thousand patients at a time live within the community with local families and work on everyday tasks until they are well.

Because of the madness of her father, Dymphna is known as the patroness of mental and nervous afflictions. It is assumed she was sexually abused; thus she is also the patroness of incest victims and runaways. Saint Dymphna is traditionally pictured with the palms of martyrdom. In some images she is depicted with the sword that beheaded her, and the devil, representing mental illness, is shown in chains at her feet.

Her feast day is May 15.

the NOVENA

O God, *we humbly beseech you through your servant Saint Dymphna, who sealed with her blood the love she bore you, to grant relief to those who suffer from mental afflictions and nervous disorders, especially* (name the afflicted person)

Saint Dymphna, helper of the mentally afflicted, pray for us.

Saint Dymphna, comforter of the despondent, pray for us.

Saint Dymphna, renowned for many miracles, please hear my plea. Amen.

(Recite one Glory Be)

**Say this novena nine times in a row
for nine days in a row.**

St. Rita of Cascia

1377–1447

ABUSED WIFE, MOTHER, WIDOW, AND NUN, Saint Rita experienced her earthly life on many different levels. Because of this, she is invoked more frequently than the Virgin Mary in many regions of the world. Her novena is said to work miracles in impossible situations. Because of her own terrible marriage, it is particularly effective in the case of marital difficulties.

Her very name, Rita, was a divine gift. Before she was born, an angel visited her mother and gave her this name from God. She was the only child of an older couple who owned a farm in Roccaporena, near Spoleto, in Italy. As a child, she had an overwhelming desire to become a nun. Instead, she acquiesced to her parents' wishes and entered into an arranged marriage at the age of twelve. Her husband proved to be violent and promiscuous. She had two sons with him and never wavered in her devotion to God or duty to her family. She withstood eighteen years of this abuse and public humiliation. One day, overcome with remorse, her husband repented to her over the miserable life she had endured at his hands. A few weeks later, he was brought home dead, murdered in a vendetta. Her two sons, who had much of their father's character, wanted to violently avenge his killing. Saint Rita prayed that they would never stain their souls with the sin of murder. Before they could take any action, they were both stricken with a fatal illness. While dying, they made peace with their mother. Rita was thirty years old. All she had previously lived for was now gone.

Sancta Rita a Cascia

*O you who shine as a star of hope
in the midst of darkness, blessed Saint
Rita, bright mirror of God's grace,
in patience and fortitude you are a
model of all the states in life.*

Being alone in the world and so devout, she tried to join the local Augustinian convent. Because they only accepted virgins, she was turned away three times. It was at this last refusal that her mystical powers began to reveal themselves. Three saints whom she always prayed to—Saint John the Baptist, Saint Nicholas of Tolentino, and Saint Augustine—appeared to her in her sleep and insisted that she return to the convent. The nuns received her with overwhelming support and she was admitted to that order in 1407. She devoted herself to taking care of the older sick nuns. In her lifetime, Saint Rita was known for the power of her prayers. It was said she could make the impossible happen. She was especially impressed with Christ's passion and meditated on the crown of thorns he wore while being crucified. She begged to feel a part of Christ's suffering. Suddenly, one of the thorns from the crucifix struck her on the forehead. It left a deep wound that never healed. Her image is always depicted with this thorn in her head, with the rays of mystical experience shooting out.

Saint Rita died of tuberculosis in 1447. She is often shown with roses, because at her death the roses in her garden bloomed off-season so that they could be used to adorn her casket. Her body lies incorrupt in an elaborate tomb in the little city of Cascia. This shrine, which still survives, was the scene of countless miracles and answered prayers. Because so many women can identify with her difficult life, she is a much-sought-after patron in Italy, Spain, France, Ireland, South America, and the Philippines.

Her feast day is May 22.

the
NOVENA

O holy protectress of those who art in greatest need, O you who shine as a star of hope in the midst of darkness, blessed Saint Rita, bright mirror of God's grace, in patience and fortitude you are a model of all the states in life. I unite my will with the will of God through the merits of my Savior, Jesus Christ, and in particular through his patient wearing of the crown of thorns, which with tender devotion you daily contemplated. Through the merits of the holy Virgin Mary and your own graces and virtues, I ask you to obtain my earnest petition, provided it be for the greater glory of God and my own sanctification. Guide and purify my intention, O holy protectress and advocate, so that I may obtain the pardon of all my sins and the grace to persevere daily, as you did in walking with courage, generosity, and fidelity down the path of life.

(Mention your request.)

Saint Rita, advocate of the impossible, pray for us.

Saint Rita, advocate of the helpless, pray for us.

(Recite Our Father, Hail Mary, and Glory Be three times each.)

**Say this novena nine times in a row
for nine days in a row.**

St. Paul the Apostle

First Century

OF ALL THE SAINTS IN THIS BOOK, SAINT Paul offers the greatest example of a life totally transformed in an instant by the intercession of divine grace. Saint Paul was once a zealous persecutor devoted to hunting down and imprisoning Christians whose conversion was so extreme that it is commemorated by its own feast day, January 25. Bitten by snakes, stoned by mobs, tortured, and shipwrecked, Saint Paul was left for dead many times. He is known as the Great Apostle because of his unstoppable energy and the success of his missionary journeys. Told to preach to the heathen nations and non-Jews, he is known as the doctor of the gentiles because he traveled throughout Greece and Asia Minor converting thousands. He is invoked for strength, patience, and faith. His numerous writings and long sojourns make him the patron saint of journalists and public relations.

Born a Roman citizen at Tarsus in Cilicia, his given name was Saul. His father, a devout man, sent him to study under the famous rabbi Gamaliel in Jerusalem. As a young man Paul was a model Pharisee, the most extreme of all the Jewish sects, and zealous in his pursuit and persecution of Christians. He firmly believed that the only way to preserve Jewish law was to wipe the Christians off the face of the earth and he was present at the stoning death of Saint Stephen, the first martyr. Ten months after Christ was crucified, Paul was on his way to Damascus to arrest Christians when he was blinded by light and fell from his horse. While on the ground a voice asked him, "Saul, Saul, why

*We expect everything from your prayers to
the divine master and to Mary, queen of the
apostles. Grant, O doctor of the gentiles, that we
may live by faith, save ourselves by hope, and
that charity alone reign in us . . .*

dost thou persecute me?" When Paul replied, "Who art thou Lord?" The voice answered, "Jesus of Nazareth." Paul was then told to continue to Damascus and await instructions. Paul spent the next three days unable to see or eat. It was during this time that he says he learned the Gospel. The entire teachings were infused in him. When he regained his vision on the fourth day, he was baptized and changed his name from Saul, the name of a great king, to Paul, which means small as a sign of humility.

Because of his reputation as a persecutor, Paul was at first mistrusted by the original apostles. After three years in Damascus, his former allies in the synagogue were so incensed with his new preachings that he had to be lowered over the city walls in a basket in the dark of night to escape death. When he returned to Jerusalem twelve years later he was arrested for creating chronic havoc and, because of his Roman citizenship, he was deported to Rome for a trial. He survived shipwreck off Malta and was released in Rome. He then traveled to Spain and Ephesus and was arrested once again for his revolutionary preachings. He was brought back to Rome and beheaded in A.D. 67 in a place called Tre Fontane, Three Fountains, so named because it was said that Saint Paul's head bounced three times when it was cut off and in each place it bounced a fountain sprang from the earth. His body is buried in the basilica of Saint Paul in Rome. Saint Paul is also the patron saint of Malta, evangelists, and snake bite.

the
NOVENA

O holy apostle who, with your teachings and with your charity, taught the entire world, look kindly upon us, your children and disciples.

We expect everything from your prayers to the divine master and to Mary, queen of the apostles. Grant, O doctor of the gentiles, that we may live by faith, save ourselves by hope, and that charity alone reign in us. Obtain for us, O vessel of election, willing correspondence to divine grace, so that it may always remain fruitful in us. Grant that we may ever better know you, love you, and imitate you, that we may be living members of the Church, the mystical body of Jesus Christ. Raise up many and holy apostles. May the warm breath of true charity permeate the entire world. Grant that all may know and glorify God and the divine master, way and truth and life. Obtain for me the special favors I am asking during this novena.

Lord Jesus, you know we have no faith in our own powers; in your mercy grant that we may be defended against all adversity, through the powerful intercession of Saint Paul, our teacher and father.

Say this novena nine times in a row for nine days in a row.

St. Anthony of Padua

1195–1231

ALWAYS DEPICTED WITH THE BABY JESUS, Saint Anthony of Padua is the most popular saint in the world. The unconditional love and kindness that are the essence of Saint Anthony's nature are best represented by this story. While walking through his garden, an older relative heard the giggling and laughing of a baby. He looked up to see Anthony with the baby Jesus in his arms, happily carrying him and talking to him. The baby kissed Anthony and disappeared. In his novena, we beg Saint Anthony to whisper our request to the infant. Since babies are not judgmental, this incarnation of Christ will surely grant our petitions. Because of this special relationship, Saint Anthony is approachable by all, for large and small favors alike.

Born in Lisbon, Portugal, to noble parents, he was baptized Fernando. He took the name Anthony upon entering the Franciscan order. He intended to preach in Morocco and, if necessary, die a martyr for his faith. Instead, after arriving there, he became very ill and was sent home. His ship was blown off course and he ended up in Messina, Sicily. He then attended the great meeting of all Franciscans, where he was very moved to be seated next to the order's founder, Saint Francis of Assisi.

Saint Anthony was magnetic and charismatic. Sent by the Franciscans to be a traveling preacher around Lombardy and southern France, and with only prayer as preparation, he gave powerful speeches, overwhelming his audiences with his love for a more spiritual life. Saint Anthony was

O gentle and loving Saint Anthony,
whose heart was ever filled with human
sympathy, whisper my petition into the
ears of the sweet infant Jesus, who loved
to be folded in your arms.

based in Padua, Italy, but he attracted huge crowds wherever he went. Many swore he radiated a holy aura.

Saint Anthony spent the last few years of his life working to help relieve the burden of debt from the poor of Padua. Saint Anthony's Bread, devoted to feeding the hungry, is a charity that is still in existence. After their novena prayers are answered, many people make donations to this organization in thanks.

Worn out by his travels, Saint Anthony died at the age of thirty-six. His reputation for compassion was so legendary that even a few weeks after his death, when a child drowned in the river and the child's mother cried out to Saint Anthony in anguish, the child miraculously came back to life. Due to the many other miracles and answered prayers that followed his death, his consecration as a saint is the quickest on record, taking only one year.

Saint Anthony, credited with an extraordinary range of intercessionary powers and known as "the Wonder Worker," is most famous as the saint of lost articles. After a novice borrowed his psalter and failed to return it, Saint Anthony prayed to get the book back. The novice then had a terrifying heavenly vision that forced him to return it. In 1263, when Saint Anthony's tomb was reopened, it was found that his tongue had never decomposed. His tongue, jawbones, and vocal cords are on display in the cathedral at Padua. He is the patron saint of lost articles, the patron saint of the poor, and the patron saint of Portugal. Saint Anthony is always depicted with the infant Jesus, his returned psalter, and lilies to represent his purity.

His feast day is June 13.

the
N O V E N A

O holy Saint Anthony, gentlest of saints, your love for God and charity for his creatures made you worthy, when on earth, to possess miraculous powers. Miracles waited on your word, which were ever ready to speak for those in trouble or anxiety. Encouraged by this thought, I implore of you to obtain for me (mention your request). *The answer to my prayer may require a miracle; even so, you are the saint of miracles. O gentle and loving Saint Anthony, whose heart was ever full of human sympathy, whisper my petition into the ears of the sweet infant Jesus, who loved to be folded in your arms, and the gratitude of my heart will be ever yours.*

(Recite one Our Father, one Hail Mary, one Glory Be.)

This novena is said every Tuesday in church.
Say this novena nine times in a row in front
of a lit votive candle to Saint Anthony.
It must be done nine weeks in a row.

St. Maria Goretti

1890–1902

BECAUSE OF HER GENTLE NATURE, SAINT Maria Goretti has been called the Saint Agnes of the twentieth century; but unlike the ancient girl martyrs before her, Saint Maria Goretti was not a heroic victim of the state. Murdered for refusing to submit to rape, her tragic fate was transformed into a remarkable example of the healing power of forgiveness. It is the amazing work that she accomplished after her death that caused her to be canonized as a saint in 1950. Through her intercession, her unrepentant killer became living proof of the power of love and forgiveness to transform an individual. His visions of Maria offering him flowers so moved him that his testimony became crucial in her canonization. Saint Maria Goretti is the patroness of rape victims and young girls. She is called upon for comfort, strength, and guidance. She is particularly sympathetic to the plight of young teenagers in the face of peer pressure. Her own story is an illustration of how great good can supplant evil.

Maria Goretti was born in Ancona, Italy, in 1890. She was the third of six children. Her family moved to Nettuno, where her father worked as a field hand. His death of malaria in 1900 left the family destitute, forcing his wife to take his place in the fields while Maria stayed home and cared for the younger children. Alessandro Serenelli, the twenty-year-old son of a neighboring farmer, began pestering Maria while her mother was away at work. Not wanting to cause trouble for his family, she rebuffed him as best she could, without telling anyone. On the evening of

SANTA MARIA GORETTI
Martire della Purità

*Look graciously on the unhappy human race
that has strayed far from the path of eternal
salvation. Teach us all, and especially our
youth, the courage and promptness that will
help us avoid anything that could offend Jesus.*

St. Maria Goretti

July 5, 1902, as she sat mending a shirt and minding her baby sister, Alessandro burst in and dragged Maria into the bedroom. She refused his sexual advances and he stabbed her fourteen times, leaving her for dead. She was found by family members and rushed to a hospital, where she clung to life for another twenty hours, during which time she expressed great concern for the plight of her mother and also for the soul of Alessandro Serenelli. She said that she fully forgave him and that she wanted him to be with her in paradise. Maria Goretti died immediately after making this statement. She was just eleven and a half years old. Unrepentant, Serenelli was convicted and sentenced to thirty years in prison. In the eighth year of his incarceration he had a vision of Maria standing in a garden, dressed in white with an armful of lilies. Smiling at him lovingly, she beckoned him and encouraged him to take the flowers. As he accepted them, each lily transformed into a still white flame. Stricken with remorse, Alessandro became totally devoted to the memory of the girl he had murdered. When he was released from prison in 1930, the first thing he did was beg Maria Goretti's mother for forgiveness.

The story of Maria Goretti's forgiving words became world famous. Soon after her death people began to pray to her for strength and guidance. Many, along with Serenelli, attested to her positive intervention. Her cult became so popular that there were 250,000 people crowded into Vatican Square on the day of her canonization. Saint Maria Goretti is shown with the martyr's palms and her bouquet of lilies.

HER FEAST DAY IS JULY 6.

the NOVENA

Saint Maria Goretti, strengthened by God's grace, you did not hesitate, even at the age of eleven, to sacrifice life itself to defend your virginal purity. Look graciously on the unhappy human race that has strayed far from the path of eternal salvation. Teach us all, and especially our youth, the courage and promptness that will help us avoid anything that could offend Jesus. Obtain for me a great horror of sin, so that I may live a holy life on earth and win eternal glory in heaven. Please intercede for me in obtaining the favor I now ask. Amen.

(Mention your request.)

(Recite one Our Father, one Hail Mary, one Glory Be.)

**Say this novena nine times in a row
for nine days in a row.**

St. Ann & St. Joachim

First Century B.C.

NOVENAS TO SAINTS JOACHIM AND ANN, as the parents of the Virgin Mary and the grandparents of Jesus Christ, are known for their intense power. Having suffered almost every trial a couple on earth may experience, they are approachable for the solving of any family crisis. Shamed by infertility, they were married for twenty years before they had their only child. They faced their daughter's unexpected pregnancy and her near-desertion by her fiancé with great faith and tolerance. After Saint Joachim died, Saint Ann, in the throes of widowhood, watched as her beloved grandson became a prisoner and was crucified. Saints Joachim and Ann offer the loving acceptance and wisdom of grandparents, and one should never be ashamed to turn to them for any reason.

Very little factual information is available about the parents of the Virgin Mary. Saint Ann is said to have been twenty years old when she married the forty-nine-year-old Joachim. Comfortable financially, they lived in Nazareth and were faithful followers of the Jewish religion. Each year they divided their income into thirds, offering the first part to the temple for the worship of God, distributing the second to the poor, and keeping the third to maintain their moderate lifestyle. Their great misfortune was their barrenness. At the time, this was considered a divine punishment, and it led ultimately to Joachim's offering being refused at the temple. Their community began to snub them, considering them inferior. Both Ann and Joachim made a vow to the Lord that if they did have a child, they would conse-

O divine Savior, we thank you for having chosen Saints Joachim and Ann to be the parents of our Blessed Mother Mary and so to be your own beloved grandparents. We place ourselves under their patronage this day.

crate it to his service. After twenty years of marriage and no children, and once again humiliated when his offering to the temple was rejected, Joachim, too ashamed to return home, went to live among his shepherds. There, an angel came to him, ordered him to return to his wife, and told him that she was pregnant, saying, "Delayed conceptions and infertile childbearing are all the more wonderful! Your wife will bear you a daughter and you will call her Mary. As you have vowed, she will be consecrated to the Lord from infancy and filled with the Holy Spirit from her mother's womb." Simultaneously, Saint Ann had been given the same news. She gave birth to the Virgin Mary at the age of forty. Saint Joachim was sixty-nine. Devoted to God, they raised Mary accordingly. True to their promise, they sent her to live in the temple to serve God when she was three years old. This was an extremely difficult act of faith on their part, surrendering the one thing they cherished most to God. So it was that Mary never lived among common people. She was given extraordinary parents and a sheltered, religious life in the service of God.

Saint Ann is the better known of the two saints, and her cult goes back to the beginning of the church. She is the patroness of housewives and women in labor. Because she kept her home in perfect order, she is also the patroness of cabinetmakers. In Brittany, Saint Ann has an exalted place. There were many sightings of her there in the 1600s. She is also the patroness of Canada.

TOGETHER, SAINTS ANN AND JOACHIM
ARE THE PATRON AND PATRONESS OF
PARENTS AND GRANDPARENTS.
THEIR FEAST DAY IS JULY 26.

the
NOVENA

Saints Joachim and Ann, grandparents of Jesus and parents of Mary, we seek your intercession. We beg you to direct all our actions to the greater glory of God and the salvation of souls. Strengthen us when we are tempted, console us during our trials, help us when we are in need, be with us in life and in death.

O divine Savior, we thank you for having chosen Saints Joachim and Ann to be the parents of our Blessed Mother Mary and so to be your own beloved grandparents. We place ourselves under their patronage this day. We recommend to them our families, our children, and our grandchildren. Keep them from all spiritual and physical harm. Grant that they may ever grow in greater love of God and others.

Saints Joachim and Ann, we have many great needs. We beg you to intercede for us before the throne of your divine Grandson. All of us here have our own special intentions, our own special needs, and we pray that through your intercession our prayers may be granted. Amen.

(Mention your request.)

**Say this novena nine times in a row
for nine days in a row.**

St. Alphonsus Liguori

1696–1787

CRIPPLED BY ARTHRITIS AND READY TO die at age seventy-two, Saint Alphonsus Liguori went on to live another nineteen years, publishing over sixty books and writing poetry and music. His disease made him so conscious of his mortality that he assumed each day was his last and lived accordingly. He is the patron of those suffering from arthritis and the pains of old age. He sets the example of turning suffering to an advantage. In his case, his ill health made him use his earthly time in the most efficient manner. Saint Alphonsus Liguori is most frequently invoked for a cure to illness, and if that is not possible, for a way to bear illness in the most productive way. It is also thought that those who suffer physical torments on earth and offer those pains as reparations for the sins of mankind have more intercessionary power after death than others. Because he spent so many years of his life in chronic pain, unable even to lift his chin off of his chest, Saint Alphonsus is thought to be an extremely effective intercessionary force.

Born near Naples, Italy, in 1696, Alphonsus Liguori started out in life as a brilliant lawyer. A doctor of law by the age of sixteen, he practiced for eight years before losing his first case. He always attributed his success at law to his daily attendance of mass. His first loss in court—the result of an oversight on his part—came as a devastating blow to him. Humiliated, he fasted and prayed for three days. While doing charitable works in the Hospital for the Incurables, he found himself surrounded by mysterious light. The building seemed to rock and an interior voice said,

*Glorious Saint Alphonsus, loving father of
the poor and sick, all your life you devoted
yourself with a charity really heroic to
lightening their spiritual and bodily miseries.*

"Leave the world and give yourself to me." This occurred twice. A few years later, in 1726, he was ordained a priest. He devoted himself to working in the poorest areas of Naples and developed a reputation as a popular preacher. Though a highly educated professional, able to argue the smallest nuance in law and theology, Saint Alphonsus said, "I have never preached a sermon that the poorest old woman in the congregation could not understand." His confessional was always crowded, and he is credited with healing a great number of hardened sinners. Saint Alphonsus founded the order of Redemptorist fathers, dedicated to going out among the poorest neighborhoods. He wanted his priests to preach practical sermons and act as missionaries, bringing the word of God to the forgotten. At the age of sixty-six, Saint Alphonsus was made the bishop of Saint Agata, a diocese of thirty thousand people. When ill health forced him to be bedridden, the Pope refused to accept his resignation because he felt that the power of Alphonsus's prayers would help his constituents more than the actual good works of anyone else. Saint Alphonsus lived in very troubled times. In 1775 he was forced to leave the Redemptorist order he had founded because of a document he had mistakenly signed. The order was split in two and he died before it was reunited. Saint Alphonsus Liguori died in 1787 at the age of 91.

In art he is always depicted with his chin on his chest due to his arthritic condition. In this image he shelters a baby as he charitably assists an elderly beggar in honor of his mission to the poor.

the
NOVENA

Glorious Saint Alphonsus, loving father of the poor and sick, all your life you devoted yourself with a charity really heroic to lightening their spiritual and bodily miseries. Full of confidence in your tender pity for the sick, since you yourself have patiently borne the cross of illness, I come to you for help in my present need.

(Mention your request.)

Loving father of the suffering, Saint Alphonsus, whom I invoke as the Arthritis Saint, since you suffered from this disease in your lifetime, look with compassion upon me in my suffering. Beg God to give me good health. If it is not God's will to cure me, then give me strength to bear my cross patiently and to offer my sufferings in union with my crucified Savior and his Mother of Sorrows, for the glory of God and the salvation of souls, in reparation for my sins and those of others, for the needs of this troubled world, and for the souls in purgatory.

(Recite one Our Father, one Hail Mary, one Glory Be.)

Saint Alphonsus, patron of the sick, pray for me. Amen.

Say this novena nine times in a row for nine days in a row.

St. Theresa
of Lisieux

1873–1897

ALSO KNOWN AS SAINT THERESA OF THE
Child Jesus and Saint Theresa the Little Flower, Saint
Theresa's story offers proof that one need not live a dra-
matic existence for holiness to be recognized. Cloistered in
a Carmelite convent twelve miles from her home, her life
was short and she died at the age of twenty-four. Pope Pius
X called Theresa of Lisieux "the greatest saint of modern
times." Novenas to Saint Theresa of Lisieux are particularly effective for dissolving bitter feelings or resentment.
Her belief in God was so ardent and loving that a childlike
grace and joy extend to all who invoke her. She offers the
simplicity, clarity, and innate wisdom of a kindly child.
Saint Theresa of Lisieux is prayed to by millions every day
and her statue stands in thousands of churches. How
could this unknown middle-class girl attain such international renown in so short a period of time?

The youngest of five daughters, Thérèse Martin was born
at Alençon in France. Her mother died when she was four,
and her father moved the family to Lisieux, where his late
wife's brother and sister-in-law lived. She was a beautiful
and pampered child. The household was an extremely devout one, and when her two older sisters entered the local
Carmelite convent, Thérèse yearned to follow them.

Upon entering the Carmelite order at the unusually young
age of fifteen, Thérèse Martin declared her intention: "I
want to be a saint." Her life in the order, devoted to prayer,
was unremarkable, and she spent her days doing low-level

Most gracious Little Rose Queen,
remember your promises of never letting
any request made to you go unanswered,
of sending down a shower of roses, and
of coming down to earth to do good.

chores and following the regimen of prayer. It was her dream to go to Hanoi as a missionary nun, but this desire was never realized. In 1895 she was instructed to write the story of her childhood by her mother superior. This is a common practice in cloistered convents and monasteries. A year later she became seriously ill with tuberculosis and was bedridden. She finished her book, *The Story of a Soul,* a few weeks before her death. This account of her life presents a very human, moody, middle-class girl with an ardent love for God. Writing with the knowledge that her own death is imminent, she promises that she "wants to spend her time in heaven doing good upon the earth."

Published in 1898 with a first printing of two thousand copies, *The Story of a Soul* became a spectacular success and is one of the best-selling books of the twentieth century, selling millions of copies in thirty-eight languages. After the book's publication, countless miracles were attributed to the heavenly intercession of Theresa, and a devout following of this unknown nun sprang up in all parts of the world. Because of this international influence, Saint Theresa of Lisieux is patroness of missionaries.

Her book also presented her cultivating a childlike, loving spirituality, thus making her very sympathetic to the needs and concerns of children. Roses are her symbol and she is always depicted with them. In her book she promises to "let fall from heaven a shower of roses." A heavenly sign that novena requests to Saint Theresa will be granted is the sight or smell of roses. Saint Theresa of Lisieux was canonized on May 17, 1925, and declared to be the second patron saint of France.

Her feast day is October 1.

the
NOVENA

Saint Theresa of the Child Jesus, during your short life on earth you became a mirror of angelic purity, of love strong as death, and of wholehearted abandonment to God. Now that you rejoice in the reward of your virtue, turn your eyes of mercy upon me, for I put all my confidence in you.

Obtain for me the need to keep my heart and mind pure and clean like your own, and to abhor sincerely whatever may in any way tarnish the glorious virtue of purity, so dear to our Lord.

Most gracious Little Rose Queen, remember your promises of never letting any request made to you go unanswered, of sending down a shower of roses, and of coming down to earth to do good. Full of confidence in your power with the Sacred Heart, I implore your intercession in my behalf and beg of you to obtain the request I so ardently desire.

(Mention your request.)

Holy little Theresa, remember your promise to do good upon the earth and shower down your roses on those who invoke you. Obtain for me from God the graces I hope for from his infinite goodness. Let me feel the powers of your prayers in every need. Give me consolation in all the bitterness of this life, and especially at the hour of death, that I may be worthy to share eternal happiness with you in heaven. Amen.

**Say this novena nine times in a row
for nine days in a row.**

St. Francis of Assisi

1182–1226

ARDENT LOVE FOR EVERYTHING IN THE universe so consumed Saint Francis of Assisi that he refused to have a full tonsure shaved into his head so that bugs and vermin, his "more simple brethren," might still have a home in his hair. He called all animals brother and sister and exhorted every creature to honor its creator. It is said that birds became quiet when he preached and that when he walked through their flocks, they never moved unless he asked it of them. A great poet, Saint Francis himself wrote the first part of this novena. Because of the mystical way he experienced the world, in full possession of and living in divine light, he is invoked to change our view of the world and fill our lives with grace.

He was born Giovanni Bernadone in the town of Assisi in the year 1182. His father was a wealthy cloth merchant and an upstanding member of the local upper classes. Everyone called him Francesco instead of Giovanni because his mother was from Provence and he was given to exclaiming in French. Francis lived a pleasure-filled life as a young man, and it was assumed he would inherit his father's business and social position. When war broke out with neighboring Perugia, Francis went to fight, viewing it all as a great adventure. He was taken prisoner, however, and eventually returned to his family extremely ill. As he recovered, his old way of life seemed to bore him. It was in the neglected Church of San Damiano that he heard the crucifix speak to him: "Go and repair my house, which you see is falling down." He took these instructions literally,

S. FRANCISCUS ASSISIENSI

© PEKA
4/208
Germany

Lord, make me an instrument of your peace.
Where there is hatred, let me sow love; Where there is
injury, pardon; Where there is doubt, faith; Where
there is despair, hope; Where there is darkness, light;
And where there is sadness, joy.

enraging his father. Ultimately, he renounced his inheritance, throwing his clothes into the street. The bishop of Assisi provided Francis with his new garments, the brown robe of a monk.

Living alone, Saint Francis rebuilt San Damiano, sometimes begging for the money for supplies. He was eventually joined by a few other young men of his status, and in 1209 he wrote his first holy rule. He embraced poverty and was intent on living as the original apostles of Christ did, traveling, preaching, and begging for alms. When he prayed, the bright light in his raptures caused him to cry, but he could not bear to stop. His followers, worried that he would ruin his eyesight, attempted to intervene, but he replied, "We are the same as the flies, attracted to light." In 1224, while praying alone on the secluded mountain of La Verna, Francis became the first saint to know the suffering of the crucified Christ by receiving the stigmata. These wounds stayed with him for the remaining two years of his life.

Saint Francis of Assisi is one of the greatest saints of the Catholic Church and is the founder of the Franciscan friars. Yet so true was his embrace of humility that he himself was never ordained a priest, only a deacon. He lived out his life in the order he founded as a humble member with no official status. He was canonized a saint in 1228. Because of his extensive travels in his native country and his love for its natural beauty, Saint Francis is the Patron Saint of Italy.

HIS FEAST DAY IS OCTOBER 4.

the
NOVENA

Lord, make me an instrument of your peace.
Where there is hatred, let me sow love;
Where there is injury, pardon;
Where there is doubt, faith;
Where there is despair, hope;
Where there is darkness, light;
And where there is sadness, joy.

O divine master,
Grant that I may not so much seek
to be consoled as to console,
to be understood as to understand,
to be loved as to love.

For it is in giving that we receive,
in pardoning that we are pardoned, and in
dying that we are born to Eternal Life. Amen.

☩

Saint Francis of Assisi, reflection of Christ
through your life of poverty and humility, grant
us through your intercession the graces we so
much need for soul and body. Especially during
this novena, we ask for (mention your request). *We*
also ask your blessings on all those whom we
love. Amen.

It is particularly effective the nine days before
October 4, the feast day of Saint Francis of Assisi.
Say this novena nine times in a row
for nine days in a row.

St. Gerard Majella

1725–1775

Saint Gerard Majella is an example of a hidden life revealed. Gardener, porter, tailor, and sacristan, he is known as "the Wonder Worker of the Eighteenth Century" due to the amazing mystical gifts he displayed in the last three years of his very short life. Always humble in his daily duties, Gerard was so intuitive that he could read into the hearts and souls of those around him. There are many novenas to Saint Gerard, but the most popular is the prayer for motherhood. His heightened sensitivity made his prayers for the health of pregnant women, women in labor, and those wanting to conceive children extremely successful. For this reason he is the patron saint of expectant mothers. He is invoked by women hoping to get pregnant as well as for a healthy pregnancy and safe delivery.

Saint Gerard was born at Muro, south of Naples. According to his mother, he was the perfect child, always devout. His father was a tailor who died when Gerard was twelve. Supporting his mother and three sisters made him very sympathetic to the needs and sorrows of women. He was apprenticed to a tailor who constantly berated him. He then served as a house servant in the home of the bishop of Lacedogna. In poor health, Gerard asked for permission to enter the order of the Capuchin friars but was refused. He returned home, where he spent much of his day in prayer. Because of his mystical gifts and generosity, Saint Alphonsus Liguori, the founder of the Redemptorists, invited him into that order as a lay brother in 1752. Once, while visit-

SANCTUS
GERARDO MAIELLA C.SS.R.

PEKA
63 4/266
Germany

*Beseech the Master of Life, from whom all
paternity proceedeth, to render me fruitful in
offspring, that I may raise up children to God
in this life and heirs to the Kingdom of
His glory in the world to come.*

ing a family, he dropped his handkerchief as he was leaving. A woman picked it up and tried to hand it to him. He told her, "Keep it. One day it will be of service to you." Although puzzled, she did keep it. A few years later, she faced life-threatening complications while giving birth. Remembering the handkerchief and Saint Gerard's promise, she had it brought to her and held it to her womb. Immediately all the complications ceased and she gave birth to a healthy baby. Thus, this miraculous bit of cloth was passed from mother to mother whenever someone was about to give birth. By the time Saint Gerard was canonized in 1904, only a shred was left. This relic is still used today to pass the miraculous grace of Saint Gerard onto other handkerchiefs.

The greatest challenge of Saint Gerard's life occurred when he was accused by a young girl of having an affair with another young woman. He never defended himself against the charges and quietly accepted the punishment meted out by his order. A few months later the girl recanted and admitted she had made the story up. When asked why he never defended himself, Gerard said that silence is what he felt was required in the face of unjust accusations. He had always accepted his fate in life and saw no reason to change his behavior now.

In art Gerard Majella is shown with lilies for purity. His charity, obedience, and selfless service also make him the patron saint of lay brothers. He died of tuberculosis in the monastery at Avellino. He was twenty-nine years old.

the
NOVENA

PRAYER FOR MOTHERHOOD

O good Saint Gerard, powerful intercessor before God and Wonder Worker of our day, I call upon you and seek your aid. You who on earth always fulfilled God's design, help me to do the holy will of God. Beseech the Master of Life, from whom all paternity proceeds, to render me fruitful in offspring, that I may raise up children to God in this life and heirs to the Kingdom of his glory in the world to come. Amen.

Dear Mother Mary, speak to Jesus for me.

**Say this novena nine times in a row
for nine days in a row.**

St. Jude

First Century

SAINT JUDE, "HELPER OF THE HOPELESS," is one of the most invoked saints of our century. He is the saint of the impossible, and it is said that he never fails to bring relief to those in desperate need. We turn to Saint Jude when all else fails. The flame of the Holy Spirit always burns over his head. His is a powerful presence, ever ready to step in and take control of a desperate situation. Because he was ever faithful to Christ and with him at the very beginning, he is in an especially exalted state of grace and can easily negate all common trials and tribulations.

Jude Thaddeus was one of the original Twelve Apostles. Brother of James the Lesser and a cousin of Jesus, he grew up with Christ and played with him as a child. He is venerated in France and in Rome, where his relics are located; but devotion to Saint Jude all but disappeared in the early Middle Ages. Because he was often confused with Judas Iscariot, the apostle who betrayed Christ, no one ever invoked Saint Jude for anything. This is why he became the saint of the impossible. In order to have people invoke him, he helped those in the most difficult circumstances. When a request is granted, the person praying must publish his thanks to Saint Jude. This way, more people will know to call on him. Daily and weekly newspapers are filled with small ads thanking him for his intercession.

In his time Saint Jude Thaddeus was known for his greatness of heart. It is said that he was so kindly and spiritual in nature, he glowed. He traveled through Edessa, Meso-

S. JUDAS TADEO AP.

Do not despise my poor prayer. Do not let my trust be confounded! God has granted to you the privilege of aiding mankind in the most desperate cases. Oh, come to my aid that I may praise the mercies of God!

potamia, and Pontus preaching Christianity. Abgar, the king of Edessa, was quite impressed with him. Since this king suffered from leprosy, he was anxious to meet Jesus so that he might be cured. He invited Jesus to come and share his kingdom. When he was told that this was not possible, he commisioned an artist to draw Christ's portrait. The artist was so intimidated by the glow in Christ's eyes, he could not draw. Christ took a linen cloth and impressed it on his own face. His image came off on it, perfectly rendered. Saint Jude took this portrait back to King Abgar, who rubbed it on his body and was cured of his leprosy. This is the large image that Saint Jude wears around his neck in art.

Saint Jude is associated with Saint Simon, with whom he traveled to Persia. They were subjects of great curiosity and popularity among the people of the places they traveled. They frequently outwitted court magicians and priests, to the amusement of the local kings. Invited to have their losing antagonists executed, as was the custom of the day, the two apostles forbade this, saying they had been sent not to kill the living but to bring the dead back to life. Ultimately Saint Simon and Saint Jude were martyred in the city of Samir after enraging the local priests. Saint Jude was beaten to death with a club. This is the staff he is always shown with in art.

the NOVENA

UNFAILING PRAYER TO SAINT JUDE

Glorious apostle, Saint Jude Thaddeus, I salute you through the Sacred Heart of Jesus. Through his Heart I praise and thank God for all the graces he has bestowed upon you. I implore you, through his love, to look upon me with compassion. Do not despise my poor prayer. Do not let my trust be confounded! God has granted to you the privilege of aiding mankind in the most desperate cases. Oh, come to my aid that I may praise the mercies of God! All my life I will be your grateful client until I can thank you in heaven. Amen.

(Mention your request.)

Saint Jude, pray for us, and for all who invoke your aid.

Your request will be granted by the eighth day.
Publication of thanks to Saint Jude must be promised.
**Say this novena nine times in a row
for nine days in a row.**

St Martin de Porres

1579–1639

UNIVERSAL HEALING AND HARMONY ARE the themes of Saint Martin de Porres's life. He was so in tune with the rhythms of nature and the universe that he was able to heal any sickness, read minds, and converse with animals. To Saint Martin, physical health was essential for spiritual growth; thus, he should be called on whenever wholeness in health or personal relationships are required. Multiracial himself, he is the patron of racial harmony and invoked whenever racial tensions arise.

Saint Martin was born in Lima, Peru, just thirty-five years after the conquest of Pizarro. His father was a Spanish nobleman and his mother was a free black woman. Since people of mixed race were reviled, Saint Martin might have been just another social outcast in that country's history. Instead he became one of Peru's national idols. When Martin was twelve he was apprenticed to a barber. In those times, besides being a haircutter, a barber was also a surgeon, doctor, and pharmacist. By the time he was eighteen years old, Martin's reputation as a healer was well established. Rather than pursue his profession, Martin kept giving all of his money to the poor. His was a desire to serve God in a state of total childlike humility. He entered the local Dominican monastery as a tertiary, the lowest possible level; there he swept the floors and dreamed of being martyred in some foreign mission. Instead, his undeniable talent as a healer became obvious, and he was put in charge of the infirmary. Tirelessly working, he tended to African slaves, the native population, and the Spanish nobility with

Saint Martin de Porres, your concern and charity embraced not only your needy brethren, but also the animals of the field. You are a splendid example of charity; we thank and praise you.

the same all-consuming intensity. His power to heal any sickness was legendary, and he was so intuitive that his patients swore he could read their minds. Stories of his wondrous abilities spread and became more and more elaborate: he was seen walking through a locked door; he was seen in two places at one time; and some said he could fly from one place to another.

Because of Saint Martin's attunement to nature and its elements, animals flocked to him. He even set up a makeshift hospital to tend sick dogs and cats. Another story has it that he made a pact with the local rats and mice that he would feed them every day if they promised to stay out of the monastery. Each noon he opened the doors of the monastery and fed the poor. No matter how many hungry people were waiting, he never ran out of food.

Saint Martin's holiness and miraculous cures made him famous in his own lifetime. Bishops and learned men routinely consulted him to resolve theological problems. This fame was undoubtedly the most difficult aspect of his life, since humility and prayer were the most important things to him. Because of his earlier profession, Saint Martin de Porres is also the patron of hairdressers and barbers. In art he is often shown holding a lily for purity and a broom for humility, while standing with small animals at his feet to reflect his closeness to nature. Saint Martin de Porres died of quartan fever in 1639 when he was sixty years old. Immediately upon his burial, miraculous healings were reported all around his tomb site.

His feast day is November 3.

the NOVENA

Saint Martin de Porres, your concern and charity embraced not only your needy brethren, but also the animals of the field. You are a splendid example of charity; we thank and praise you. From above, hear the requests of your needy brethren.

(Mention your request.)

By modeling our lives after yours, and imitating your virtues, may we live content knowing that God has looked favorably upon us. Because this is so, we can accept our burdens with strength and courage in order to follow in the footsteps of our Lord and the Blessed Mother. May we reach the Kingdom of Heaven through the intercession of our Lord Jesus Christ. Amen.

Say this novena nine times in a row for nine days in a row.

St. Frances
Xavier Cabrini

1850–1917

THE MIRACLES ATTRIBUTED TO MOTHER Cabrini are ongoing. In the chapel that holds her remains in New York City, there is a constantly changing collection of plaques, gifts, thank-you cards, and written testimonials to answered prayers by those who have invoked her help. She is the first American citizen ever to be named a saint, and there are three major shrines to her in the United States. Having lived among the world's forgotten citizens and the working poor, she is especially known for her intercession in relieving the small everyday burdens and disappointments that can sometimes seem insurmountable.

She was born Maria Francesca Cabrini in the Lombard region of Italy. She lived on a farm, the youngest of thirteen children, only four of whom survived adolescence. When she was twenty years old, both her parents died in a smallpox epidemic. Due to her own ill health, she was turned down by two convents that she tried to join. Qualified as a schoolteacher, in 1880 she was sent to Codogno to run a small orphanage. There she founded the Missionary Sisters of the Sacred Heart, the first group of missionary nuns. She took the name Frances Xavier after her idol, Saint Francis Xavier, patron of the missions. It was her dream to continue his work in Asia by opening up a mission in China. After her orphanage was closed, she went to Rome and surprised many by having the rule of the order she founded authorized by the Pope in so little time. When he learned of her desire to be sent to China, he pointed out the unmet need in America, particularly New York City, where more than

O loving Savior, infinitely generous, seeking
only our interest, from your Sacred Heart
came these words of pleading love:
"Come to me all you that labor and
are burdened and I will refresh you."

fifty thousand newly emigrated Italians lived in the filthy slums. With six nuns, Mother Cabrini arrived in America in 1889, only to be told by the archbishop of New York to go home. Instead, they moved into the Italian ghetto and opened an orphanage. Within a few short years, Mother Cabrini's order opened a multitude of orphanages, schools, hospitals, and nurse's homes throughout the United States, Central America, Argentina, Brazil, France, Spain, England, and Italy, all catering to the displaced and destitute.

Mother Cabrini was gifted with an innate business sense which made her extremely successful at raising money. Thought of as a somewhat difficult personality, she was very tenacious. This is perhaps due to the nature of her ministry. She lived among the lost and abandoned and even administered to the most violent offenders in Sing-Sing prison. Her experiences with the diverse groups of people she came in contact with softened her nature. Her character mellowed and she became less narrow in her judgments. In 1909 she became an American citizen. Just as Mother Cabrini evolved as a person, she is evolving as a saint. Though she is the patroness of immigrants, orphans, displaced persons and hospital administrators, she is invoked for absolutely anything. Indeed, her popularity as an intercessionary force is growing. Mother Cabrini died of malaria on December 22, 1917, and was canonized by Pope Pius XII in 1946. Her body lies on view at the Saint Frances Cabrini Shrine in New York City.

the
NOVENA

O loving Savior, infinitely generous, seeking only our interest, from your Sacred Heart came these words of pleading love: "Come to me all you that labor and are burdened and I will refresh you." Relying on this promise of your infinite charity, we come to you and in the lowliness of our hearts earnestly beg you to grant us the favor we ask in this novena, through the intercession of your faithful servant Saint Frances Xavier Cabrini. Amen.

Say this novena nine times in a row for nine days in a row.

St. FRANCIS
Xavier

1506–1552

The life of Saint Francis Xavier, a brilliant intellectual who had to learn how to trust like a child, is an illustration of the power of grace. His special novena, the Miraculous Novena of Grace, is a tool for welcoming clarity and synchronicity into our lives. It helps us surrender control to a higher power. As he attained ever more grace through prayer, Saint Francis Xavier matured from being an earnest, sheltered college professor to becoming a man at home any place in the world, able to converse in any language, with people of all levels of society.

Born into a noble family in Aragon, Spain, Francis Xavier grew up in a castle, the youngest of six children. He was doted upon by his family, and his father was delighted when he showed an early ability to write well. Francis Xavier was then set upon an intellectual path and sent to the University of Paris to complete his education. There he displayed a considerable aptitude for philosophy, and it was thought he might even become one of the world-famous professors at the Sorbonne. His life changed course, however, when he met an older student named Ignatius Loyola. Though he took an instant dislike to Loyola, Francis Xavier eventually joined his new order of priests, the Society of Jesus, which was devoted to spreading Christ's message abroad. Saint Francis Xavier became one of the six original Jesuits and was sent to Goa in India, where the Portuguese had a colony. When he arrived there he realized how horribly degrading the European influence was on the native culture. Slavery, prostitution, thiev-

S. Franciscus Xaverius

I implore you to obtain for me,
through your powerful intercession,
the greatest of all blessings, that
of living and dying in the state of grace.

ery, and gambling were practiced openly. His beautifully written and voluminous collection of letters detailing his life in Goa and the degradation of the local people are still studied today. Though Francis Xavier was of noble birth, he was still able to relate to and empathize with the lowest-born individual. He was frequently seen chatting with prostitutes, members of the underworld, and beggars in the street. He had a miraculous ability with languages and he spoke various dialects of Indian with relative ease. His theory was to teach the simplest people first. Children loved him, as did prisoners and the outcasts of society, among whom he lived. As he devoted himself fully to his mission, Francis Xavier's gifts magnified. He is credited with the ability to speak in tongues, quiet stormy seas, heal the hopelessly ill, and predict the future.

Using Goa as a base, Francis Xavier went on to convert hundreds of thousands of people in the Far East. He was the first missionary to reach Japan, in 1544. It was his dream to go on to China, but he died, worn out from his ceaseless work, on the island of Chang-Chuen-Shan. He was forty-six years old. His body was put in quicklime and returned to Goa, where it is enshrined in an uncorrupt state. He is considered a protector by the Paravas, the indigenous people whom he saved from being decimated by both the Europeans and higher-caste Indians. Not only is he the patron saint of foreign missions; his letters make him the patron saint of writers.

HIS FEAST DAY IS DECEMBER 3.

the
NOVENA

THE MIRACULOUS NOVENA OF GRACE

Most amiable and most loving Saint Francis Xavier, in union with you I reverently adore the Divine Majesty. I rejoice exceedingly on account of the marvelous gifts which God bestowed upon you. I thank God for the special graces he gave you during your life on earth and for the great glory that came to you after your death. I implore you to obtain for me, through your powerful intercession, the greatest of all blessings, that of living and dying in the state of grace. I also beg of you to secure for me the special favor I ask in this novena. In asking this favor, I am fully resigned to the Divine Will. I pray and desire only to obtain that which is most conducive to the greater glory of God and the greater good of my soul. Amen.

(Here you may mention the grace, spiritual
or temporal, that you wish to obtain.)

(Recite one Our Father, one Hail Mary, one Glory Be.)

There are two times a year when the Miraculous Novena of Grace is considered especially powerful: from March 4 to March 12 and from November 25 to December 3.
**Say this novena nine times in a row
for nine days in a row.**

St. Barbara

Third to Fourth Century

Saint Barbara was a beautiful young girl brutally murdered by her father. Because she was avenged by God, she is invoked at times of injustice, when a fiery response is warranted or protection against violence is needed. Just as the heavenly retribution taken against her father was simple and direct, so is this novena to Saint Barbara. Though some doubt that she ever existed, Saint Barbara is one of the greatest saints of the Eastern Orthodox Catholic Church, and her statue guards countless homes and businesses. She is the saint who in spirit is most like Michael the Archangel, assuring us of universal protection and justice.

Born in the city of Nicomedia near the Persian border, her parents were wealthy and influential people who doted on their only child. It was, however, a time of considerable social upheaval. To protect his daughter from the rabble around them, Dioscurus, her father, committed her to live in a tower. From there she observed the world, entertained her friends, and was tutored by great teachers. She had much time for contemplation, and ultimately she concluded that worshipping a pantheon of gods was absurd and developed an interest in the Christian religion. While her father was away, she sent to Alexandria for the famous teacher Origen to give her further religious instruction. From him she learned about the Holy Trinity, and she was converted to Christianity. Meanwhile, her father was constructing a new bathhouse on the grounds near the tower as a present to Barbara. While visiting the site Barbara or-

*With a sword hearing your illustrious name,
Saint Barbara, I make a sign of the cross over my
heart. I pray that your spirit be my faith, that
your protection and justice be my guide, and from
all my heart, I beg that you grant this petition.*

dered the workmen to build a third window, thereby creating a symbolic unity. She also removed any pagan statues and images in the structure, replacing them with a simple cross in the wall. When her father returned from his trip, he demanded to know who had changed the bathhouse design. Barbara admitted that she had had the offending third window installed, and declared, "Grace comes to us through three channels, the Father, the Son, and the Holy Spirit." Dioscurus, infuriated to discover that his daughter was now a Christian, had her dragged off to the authorities and denounced her. Saint Barbara was then tortured for refusing to sacrifice to the pagan gods. Her own father asked to be her executioner and took out his sword and beheaded her. As he was leaving the site of her death, Dioscurus was struck by lightning and reduced to ashes. This is why Saint Barbara is invoked in the time of lightning storms, artillery bombardments, and explosions.

Saint Barbara is also invoked against sudden death and is said to bring holy communion to the faithful at the time of death. Because of her work on the bathhouse, and her affiliation with the tower in which she lived, she is also the patroness of architects. In art she is shown with her tower, holding the palms of martyrdom and the sword that beheaded her. There is a church in Cairo, Egypt, that houses her remains and is named after her. Saint Barbara was a very popular saint in France during the Middle Ages. Besides being greatly honored in Greece and Egypt, she has enjoyed a great resurgence in popularity in the Caribbean and in South America.

HER FEAST DAY IS DECEMBER 4.

the NOVENA

O Saint Barbara, I offer this prayer to you in the name of the Father, the Son, and the Holy Spirit. With a sword bearing your illustrious name, Saint Barbara, I make a sign of the cross over my heart. I pray that your spirit be my faith, that your protection and justice be my guide, and from all my heart I beg that you grant this petition. I hope to obtain this help through your grace. Amen.

(Mention your request.)

Say this novena nine times in a row for nine days in a row.

St. Lucy

285–304

CLARITY AND LIGHT ARE THE PRIMARY attributes of Saint Lucy. Often her name is invoked as a protection against temptation, since she is thought to enhance judgment and aid in discernment. The name Lucy means "light," and light is the nature of grace. Just as light shines in a direct, straight line, Saint Lucy's belief in God never wavered. Light is also immaculate, no matter how filthy the place it shines in. Her affiliation with light also extends to vision. Thus, Saint Lucy is the patron saint of the blind; we also call on her to help those with eye troubles.

Born in Syracuse, Sicily, into a noble family, Saint Lucy was secretly a Christian, having been impressed early on by the stories of Saint Agatha's martyrdom in nearby Catania. Lucy's mother suffered from long-term health problems, and Lucy took her to Saint Agatha's tomb to be healed. When her mother's health was instantly restored, she also became a Christian. Although her family had arranged for her to marry, Lucy begged to be allowed to break the engagement, as she had promised her virginity to the Lord. She wanted her dowry to be distributed to the poor and to live a life devoted to prayer and chastity. This enraged Lucy's betrothed, and he denounced her to the local authorities as a Christian and an enemy of the emperor. This being the time of the persecutions of Diocletian, the punishment for Christian beliefs was torture, then death. Lucy refused to sacrifice to the Roman idols when commanded by the local officials, saying, "The sacrifice that is pleasing

S. LUCIA

I ask you to obtain for me the grace never to consent to the temptations of the world, the flesh, and the devil, and to fight constantly against their assaults.

to God is to visit the poor and help them in their need."
Paschasius, the Roman consul, ordered her to be put in a
house of prostitution. When the soldiers came to carry
Lucy away, they could not move her. A thousand soldiers
and a thousand oxen were brought in and still she could
not be budged. Magicians and wizards chanting incanta-
tions had no effect. Paschasius, at wits' end, ordered a fire
to be built around Lucy and boiling oil to be poured on
her head. Still unfazed, Lucy said, "I have prayed for this
prolongation of my martyrdom in order to free believers
from the fear of suffering and to give unbelievers time to
insult me." At this point, a friend of the consul's plunged a
dagger into her throat and ended her earthly life. A church
was raised at the site of her death a few years later. Saint
Lucy is one of the oldest and most adored saints in the
world.

There are two different stories as to why Saint Lucy is always shown holding her eyes on a dish. One is that they
were torn from her head under torture and were then
miraculously restored. The other is that a persistent suitor
asked for her hand in marriage, citing her beautiful eyes as
the reason she won his heart. Lucy, intent on keeping her
virginity, ripped out her own eyes and sent them to him.
Here again they were miraculously restored the next day.
Saint Lucy is also always depicted with the palms of martyrdom. Her remains are partially uncorrupt and were
moved to a church in Venice. Because she died from having her throat cut, she is also invoked for throat ailments
and hemorrhages.

Her feast day is December 13.

By your steadfast faith, O glorious Saint Lucy, you firmly declared to the ruler that no one could take from you the Holy Spirit, who dwelt in your heart as in his temple. Obtain for me from God that I may always live in a holy and salutary fear of losing his grace and that I may flee everything that might cause so grievous a loss.

(Recite one Our Father, one Hail Mary, one Glory Be.)

By the great love which your immaculate spouse had for you, O glorious Saint Lucy, when by an unheard of miracle he rendered you immovable in spite of the attempts of your enemies to drag you into a place of shame and sin, I ask you to obtain for me the grace never to consent to the temptations of the world, the flesh, and the devil, and to fight constantly against their assaults by the continuous mortification of all my senses.

(Recite one Our Father, one Hail Mary, one Glory Be.)

By the same ardent love you had for Jesus, O glorious Saint Lucy, after consecrating yourself to him by an irrevocable vow, you refused profitable offers of marriage. After distributing all your goods to aid the poor, you sacrificed your life by the blade that pierced your neck. Obtain for me the grace to be filled with holy charity, that I may be ready to renounce wordly goods and endure all evil rather than become, even in the least degree, unfaithful to Jesus.

(Recite one Our Father, one Hail Mary, one Glory Be.)

The purpose of this novena is to ward off temptation and to maintain clarity in confusing situations.
**Say this novena nine times in a row
for nine days in a row.**

All Saints

When a Catholic is baptized, he or she is given a saint's name, and that saint becomes his or her patron. Also, at confirmation a saint's name is selected as one's confirmation name, preferably that of a saint one would wish to emulate.

This is a general novena to invoke the intercession of your particular saint. Novenas to your patron saint can be done at any time, but they are most appreciated on your saint's feast day. If that day is unknown to you, or you do not have a patron, November 1 has been set aside as the Day of All Saints. On this day patron saints are thanked for their protection and are asked to become more present in our lives.

The Feast of All Saints was first observed in May 609 in order to rededicate the Pantheon in Rome from a pagan temple devoted to a myriad of gods to a church known as the Blessed Mother and the Martyrs (now called Santa Maria Rotonda). Even in these early times there were thousands of saints, too many for the official calendar, and it was felt that there should be a day dedicated to them. Attendance at the ceremony was so great that the food and wine for the festivities were depleted before the celebration began. This May feast was then moved to November 1, when food supplies were more ample after the harvest.

It is said that when we honor the saints we honor ourselves. By sending them love and admiration, an amplified, magnified form of love and grace is received in return.

OMNES SANCTI ET SANCTÆ DEI
ORATE PRO NOBIS

4/135
Western, Germen

You persevered until death and gained the crown of eternal life. Remember now the dangers and confusion and anguish that surround me in my needs and troubles.

On All Saints' Day, the patrons can be prayed to individually or the saints can be universally invoked. Since the saints have had a human existence, meditating on and reflecting on their natures and lives offers the hope of improving or perfecting one's own way of being. The saints intercede for us based on their attributes and abilities. It is thought that if the saints are invoked as a group universally, they intercede for us as a group, and with such powers, it would be impossible for prayers to go unanswered. So long as it is in accordance with God's will, it is the desire of the saints to aid in the fulfillment of God's wishes.

Here the image used to illustrate the novena for All Saints represents a vision that the warden of the Church of Saint Peter was purported to have had one year after the first All Saints' Day. After he went from altar to altar imploring the help of each saint, he sat down in rapt ecstasy. Then he saw an endless procession of saints, representing every race, being led by an angel before the throne of Christ and the Virgin Mary. They sang their thanks to God for the honor done them by those on earth and they prayed for the entire world. Then the angel instructed the warden to tell the Pope what he had seen and commanded him to establish the day after the Feast of All Saints as a day for the departed souls, so that those who had no one to pray for them would be remembered as a group. Thus, the Day of All Souls is on November 2.

The Day of All Saints is November 1.

the
NOVENA

Glorious Saint _____, *my beloved patron, you served God in humility and with confidence on earth. Now you enjoy his beatific vision in heaven. You persevered until death and gained the crown of eternal life. Remember now the dangers and confusion and anguish that surround me in my needs and troubles, especially* (mention your request). *Amen.*

**Say this novena nine times in a row
for nine days in a row.**

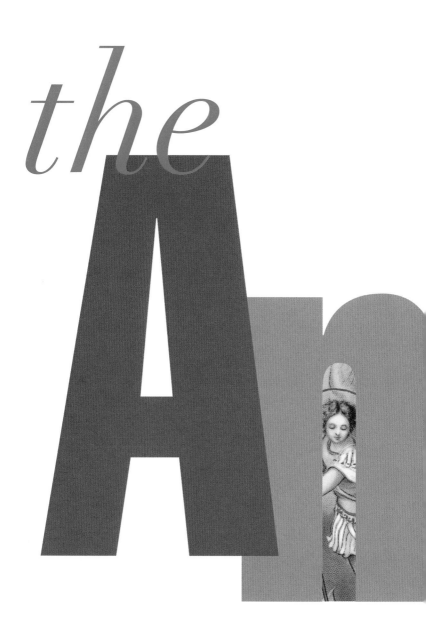

the

A

St. Raphael
Archangel

BECAUSE ANGELS HAVE NEVER HAD A HUMAN existence, their attributes are in the purest of forms. There are seven archangels that sit before the throne of God, exalted above all others. Of these, three are mentioned in the Bible as interacting the most with humanity: Raphael, Gabriel, and Michael. While entire nations invoke Michael, and Gabriel has a very specific purpose, the archangel Raphael is most effectively invoked when we are at our most human. Raphael, whose name means "Remedy of God," might also be known as the angel of everyday life. For example, we pray to Saint Raphael in hopes of meeting a life partner, before we take a trip, or to heal our illnesses. He is known for infusing even the smallest, most mundane daily events with peace and happiness.

It was Raphael who healed the earth after the fallen angels who were cast out of heaven landed on it. In ancient times there was a small body of water, akin to a pond, called Probatica. Those with devastating illnesses could go there and wait in the water as an angel of the Lord came down and, moving the water over the afflicted, healed them. That angel was Raphael. Raphael's relationship with humankind is such that he also sees to it that scientific knowledge is brought to its highest level. It was Raphael who instructed Noah on how to build the ark and King Solomon on how to build the great temple.

One of the most famous stories of Raphael's intervention is told in the Bible in the Book of Tobit. The story is significant because in it, Raphael is petitioned by disparate people, but in a wholly loving fashion he managed to

Glorious archangel Saint Raphael, great prince
of the heavenly court, you are illustrious for your
gifts of wisdom and grace. You are a guide
of those who journey by land or sea or air,
consoler of the afflicted and refuge of sinners.

St. Raphael, Archangel
is the patron saint of
Travelers Happy Meetings
The Blind The Sciences Healing

bring them all together in the most joyous of outcomes. Tobit, having gone blind and thus unable to travel with his son Tobias across the desert, called on Raphael to accompany his son. Meanwhile, on the other side of the desert was a woman named Sara who also had been praying to Raphael for relief, because she'd lost seven husbands, all of whom died on their wedding nights, victims of a demon. Raphael, disguising himself as a man named Azariah, guided Tobias in his travels. Upon reaching their destination, the angel, as Azariah, pointed Sara out to Tobias and suggested that she would make a wonderful wife. He further advised Tobias on how to defeat the demon by praying for three days, burning the innards of a fish they had caught, and thinking of God on his wedding night. Tobias and Sara were blessed with a most happy marriage, and the demon was expelled into the desert. Raphael even restored Tobit's sight. In responding to their prayers to him, Raphael was able to guide them all to a higher level of life. For this reason, prayers are said to Raphael in order to find a life partner that is on an equal spiritual level.

Saint Raphael is also the patron of travelers; we ask him not only for a safe journey, but for a more enlightened one. He is always depicted leading Tobias, who is carrying the fish. The original feast day of Raphael is October 24, but his day was changed to the Feast of the Archangel, which he shares with Gabriel and Michael, on September 29.

The Feast of the Archangel
is September 29.

the NOVENA

Glorious archangel Saint Raphael, great prince of the heavenly court, you are illustrious for your gifts of wisdom and grace. You are a guide of those who journey by land or sea or air, consoler of the afflicted, and refuge of sinners.

I beg you, assist me in all my needs and in all the sufferings of this life, as once you helped the young Tobias on his travels. Because you are the "medicine of God," I humbly pray you to heal the many infirmities of my soul and the ills that afflict my body. I especially ask of you the favor (mention your request) and the great grace of purity to prepare me to be the temple of the Holy Spirit. Amen.

**Say this novena nine times in a row
for nine days in a row.**

St. Michael Archangel

JUSTICE IN ACTION AND FIERCE PROTECTION
are requested when we call on Saint Michael the Archangel. Devotions to him predate Christianity. Three major religions—Judaism, Christianity, and Islam—consider him to be the greatest and most powerful of all angels. He is cited in the Book of Revelation as the angel who defeated Lucifer in his uprising against God. Lucifer, God's most beautiful and favored angel, insisted he was equal or superior to God. He led a band of angels in a revolt against God and his omnipotence. Michael was the standard bearer against them. He defeated Lucifer and his allies and cast them out of heaven. He then took the name Mi-cha-el, meaning "Who is like God?" The ancient Jewish people referred to Michael as "the Viceroy of Heaven" and considered him the protector of Israel. In the New Testament he is cited as the angel that will come at the end of the world to slay the Antichrist on Mount Olivet. Saint Michael was one of the three voices directing Saint Joan of Arc in her campaign to unite France. He is said to take an active role in the world and its protection and is called upon when a group, city, or nation is in danger. Also, it is Michael who meets the soul upon its earthly death and guides it to its afterlife. He is frequently shown with a pair of scales to weigh sins and virtues. This is probably why he is the patron saint of grocers.

From the earliest Christian times, the cults of devotion to Saint Michael were very popular, particularly in the East, where he was invoked to protect against illness. A church was dedicated to him in Constantinople to protect the

S. MICHAEL ARCH.

Pray for me, Saint Michael, and also for those I love. Protect us in all dangers of body and soul. Help us in our daily needs. . . . May we live a holy life, die a happy death, and reach heaven, where we may praise and love God with you forever.

St. Michael, Archangel
is the patron saint of
Grocers Soldiers Policemen
Protection against illness

health of the citizens in the fourth century. As his popularity spread, devotions to Saint Michael supplanted those to many of the pagan gods. In Germany, on the banks of the Rhine, he replaced Wotan, and in Roman Gaul he replaced Mercury. Statues depicting an angel with a battle helmet and sword began to appear in such far-flung places as India and Persia. On May 8, 492, he was sighted in a cave on the summit of Mount Gargano in southern Italy, causing it to become one of the first Christian pilgrimage sites. One hundred years later, as a plague raged in Rome, Pope Gregory I saw Michael sheathing a bloody sword over Emperor Hadrian's tomb. He took this to mean that the city was now under Michael's protection, and soon thereafter the plague ended. A church dedicated to Saint Michael was built over the tomb. It is now known as Castel Sant' Angelo (Castle of the Holy Angel). The most famous shrine to Michael is Mont-Saint-Michel in Normandy. This Benedictine abbey was founded in the tenth century to commemorate an earlier apparition.

Michael is usually shown holding a banner and a pair of scales and brandishing a sword with his foot on the neck of the devil, who is frequently represented by a dragon. Besides being the patron saint of grocers, Saint Michael is invoked to protect soldiers and policemen as well as to guard against illness. Because of the famous visions of Michael, there are local feast days to him on May 8 in Gargano and October 16 in Mont-Saint-Michel. His official feast day, the Feast of the Archangel, is September 29, which he shares with the archangels Gabriel and Raphael.

The Feast of the Archangel
is September 29.

the NOVENA

Saint Michael the Archangel, loyal champion of God and his people, I turn to you with confidence and seek your powerful intercession. For the love of God, who made you so glorious in grace and power, and for the love of the Mother of Jesus, the Queen of the Angels, be pleased to hear my prayer. You know the value of my soul in the eyes of God. May no stain of evil ever disfigure its beauty. Help me to conquer the evil spirit who tempts me. I desire to imitate your loyalty to God and Holy Mother Church and your great love for God and men. And since you are God's messenger for the care of his people, I entrust to you this special request.

(Mention your request.)

Saint Michael, since you are, by the will of the Creator, the powerful intercessor of Christians, I have great confidence in your prayers. I earnestly trust that if it is God's holy will, my petition will be granted.

Pray for me, Saint Michael, and also for those I love. Protect us in all dangers of body and soul. Help us in our daily needs. Through your powerful intercession, may we live a holy life, die a happy death, and reach heaven, where we may praise and love God with you forever. Amen.

(Recite one Our Father, one Hail Mary, one Glory Be.)

**Say this novena nine times in a row
for nine days in a row.**

St. Gabriel Archangel

COMMUNICATIONS OF ALL KINDS—IN PAR-
ticular, consolation and guidance—are the basic attributes
of the archangel Gabriel. His earthly visitations always por-
tend a major change in human history. Islam credits the
archangel Gabriel with dictating the Koran to the prophet
Mohammed. Not only does the angel Gabriel, as a divine
messenger, announce a coming event; he is also known to
explain the meaning of his news, and to those who are
frightened he offers consolation. It was Gabriel who remained with Christ on the eve of his crucifixion, giving
him the fortitude to face his fate. The name Gabriel means
"Strength from God," and thus he is invoked for courage.

The first mention of Gabriel the Archangel is in the Book
of Daniel. In it, Gabriel visits the prophet Daniel, inter-
preting his dreams and explaining his visions to him. After
Daniel prays for Israel, Gabriel goes to him and, by touch-
ing him, communicates the prophecy that "seventy weeks"
of years would elapse before the coming of the Savior. The
ancient Jews viewed the archangel Gabriel as a judgmental
figure, who meted out punishments. They believed that it
was he who buried Moses as well as leveled the cities of
Sodom and Gomorrah.

It is assumed that it was the archangel Gabriel who appeared to Saint Joachim to instruct him on the coming
birth of his daughter, Mary. To the priest Zechariah he an-
nounced the coming birth of John the Baptist. When
Zechariah scoffed at the angel because he and his wife were
too old to be parents, Gabriel struck him dumb until the
child was born. Gabriel is particularly devoted to Jesus and

Steady my resolutions, renew my courage,
comfort and console me in the problems, trials,
and sufferings of daily living as you consoled
our Savior in his agony and Mary in her
sorrows and Joseph in his trials.

the Blessed Mother and his celestial intervention occurs throughout their earthly lives. The greatest visitation of Gabriel is known as the Annunciation. He visited the fourteen-year-old Mary and told her that she would soon give birth to the Divine Savior. When Mary asked how this could be possible, since she was still a virgin, he carefully explained the role of the Holy Spirit in Christ's creation. It is said that the beauty expressed by Mary as she resigned herself to the will of God made the angel tremble. Saint Gabriel is known as "the Angel of the Incarnation" because he was present when "the Word was made flesh." As he spoke to Mary, Jesus was created in her body. Gabriel then went on to comfort and reassure Saint Joseph that this was indeed an act of God, so that he would stand by Mary. When the baby Jesus was born, it was Gabriel who spread the news of his birth to the shepherds in the surrounding region.

As Saint Raphael guides us on earth and Saint Michael meets us in death, Saint Gabriel is the angel who selects souls from heaven to be given birth in the material world. He spends the nine months that the baby is forming instructing that soul on what he or she will need to know on earth. Because of his willingness to teach and to ensure that we understand the information he imparts, Saint Gabriel is the patron of parents and teachers. His role as a heavenly messenger also makes him the patron of postal workers and of those in the communications industry. His feast day has been changed from March 24 to the Feast of the Archangel, September 29.

The Feast of the Archangel is September 29.

the
NOVENA

Saint Gabriel the Archangel, I venerate you as the Angel of the Incarnation, because God specially appointed you to bear the messages concerning the God-Man to Daniel, Zechariah, and the Blessed Virgin Mary. Give me a very tender and devoted love for the Incarnate Word and his Blessed Mother, more like your own.

I venerate you also as the "Strength from God," because you are the giver of God's strength, consoler and comforter chosen to strengthen God's faithful and teach them important truths. I ask for the grace of a special power of the will to strive for holiness of life. Steady my resolutions; renew my courage; comfort and console me in the problems, trials, and sufferings of daily living, as you consoled our Savior in his agony and Mary in her sorrows and Joseph in his trials. I put my confidence in you.

Saint Gabriel, I ask you especially for this favor: (mention your request). Through your earnest love for the Son of God made man and for his Blessed Mother, I beg of you, intercede for me that my request may be granted, if it be God's holy will.

Pray for us, Saint Gabriel the Archangel. That we may be worthy of the promises of Christ.

Say this novena nine times in a row
for nine days in a row.

The Guardian Angels

MOST OF THE WORLD'S RELIGIONS AGREE
on one thing: the presence of angels in our lives. The word
"angel" comes from the Greek word *angelos,* which means
"messenger." All angels are messengers of God. If we pray
to the saints because, having been human, they fully understand our shortcomings, we pray to the angels because
they are pure in spirit and so call us to a higher level of
being. Angels do not have human natures, and so their
perspectives are totally different from ours. We turn to
them to be reminded of the higher goal we share with
them. It is said that the more we pray to the angels, the less
the material and physical problems of the earth will seem
to matter.

Angels, who exist at the very throne of God, are said to
number in the thousands of millions. They are divided
into three hierarchies. The first is the heavenly counselors,
who are nearest to God: the seraphim, cherubim, and
thrones. They regulate the movement of light in the heav-
ens as it emanates from God. The next hierarchy is the
heavenly governors: the powers, virtues, and dominions.
These bear the conscience of all humanity, transmit divine
energy, govern the activities of all the angelic orders, and
integrate the spiritual and material world. The third hierarchy is that which has direct contact with the earth and
mankind: principalities, archangels, and angels. Each individual's guardian angel comes from this hierarchy. From
infancy until death, human life is enveloped by the watch-
ful care and intercession of the guardian angels.

By your unceasing watchfulness protect me in every
danger of soul and body. Obtain for me the grace of
final perseverance, so that after this life I may be
admitted to your glorious company and with you
may sing the praises of God for all eternity.

Pray to Guardian Angels for Spiritual perfection Grace Absolutely Anything

It is believed that each one of us has his or her own guardian angel. These angels are always with us and are responsible for keeping us on the right path, helping us rise when we fall, encouraging us to become more and more virtuous, assisting us in death, and, most important of all, acting as intermediaries, offering our prayers and good actions to God. They do not see our physical actions as much as our spiritual actions. By praying to our guardian angels, we open up a channel to the divine grace. The angels have perfect knowledge, or wisdom, and this comes from their vision of God. They are said to be endowed with blessedness from gazing enraptured at God, and this blessedness makes them view all creations and all creatures as the beautiful perfection that they really are. The more we communicate with our guardian angels, the more we become aware of our own blessedness and perfect beauty. Though angels have free will, because of this beatific existence there can be no temptation but to do God's will.

The more we pray to our guardian angels, the more sensitive we become to their advice. Intuitive thoughts and feelings become more pronounced, and we no longer rely on judgmental thinking in our decision making. We become less fearful, more accepting, more in harmony with things. This is what it means to live in a state of grace. The angels are said to be beings of light. We lighten our lives and our existence when we pray to them.

The feast day of the Guardian Angels is October 2.

the NOVENA

Bless the Lord, all you his angels. You who are mighty in strength and do his will, intercede for me at the throne of God. By your unceasing watchfulness protect me in every danger of soul and body. Obtain for me the grace of final perseverance, so that after this life I may be be admitted to your glorious company and with you may sing the praises of God for all eternity.

All you holy angels and archangels, thrones and dominions, principalities and powers and virtues of heaven, cherubim and seraphim, and especially you, my dear guardian angel, intercede for me and obtain for me the special favor I now ask. (Mention your request.)

(Recite one Glory Be.)

Say this novena nine times in a row for nine days in a row.

the Ma

Our Lady of Fatima

THE TWENTIETH CENTURY HAS BEEN THE bloodiest and most violent in the history of the world. During Mary's visits to Fatima, Portugal, in 1917, she foretold not only the terrors of the Russian Revolution and World War II, but also made a third prediction, never released, as it was judged far too terrifying. In her visits she stressed the recitation of the rosary and taking fifteen minutes to meditate on her Immaculate Heart each week. Expressing the feeling that humanity had drifted away from God, she wanted the world to offer up reparations for the disastrous state of the earth. Our Lady of Fatima is an angry and pained mother, demanding that the world come to its senses and honor its Creator. Her rules are strict. This novena is said to honor Mary and to atone for the blasphemies and ingratitude that are heaped upon God and his creations. Coming in the midst of the First World War, her warnings were pointedly political. She predicted the suffering imposed by the Communist states as well as the incredible carnage of the next world war. She strongly commanded all of humanity to pray the rosary, insisting this is the only road to peace.

On May 13, 1917, three young shepherd children, aged ten, nine, and seven—Lucia, Antonio, and Maria dos Santos—were out tending sheep at a place called Cova da Iria in Fatima. Mary appeared to them in a dazzling light, floating above the trees. She taught them how to pray the rosary and told them she would return on the thirteenth day of each month for the next five months. Though they were initially mocked for their story, a handful of people

*Most holy Virgin, who came to Fatima
to reveal to the three shepherd children the
treasures of graces hidden in the recitation
of the rosary, inspire our hearts with
a sincere love of this devotion.*

Pray to Our Lady of Fatima for Forgiveness Reparations

accompanied them when they returned to the location of Mary's visit on the thirteenth of June. There they witnessed a burst of lightning and heard the buzzing of bees. The three children stood transfixed, almost fainting with fright. By Mary's final visit, on October 13, there were seventy thousand people waiting for her to appear. It had been pouring rain for two days, and a local priest, who'd believed the children were lying, tried to disperse the crowd. In the east a bolt of lightning rang out and the rain stopped instantly. As the clouds parted, the people looking at the sun fell to their knees. It had begun to tremble and dance, and the entire crowd was engulfed by the spectrum of colors streaming from it. Some saw the face of the Virgin in the sky; others saw a huge whirling wheel of fire spinning toward the earth. The heat emanating from the rays of lights was so intense that by the end of the vision, ten minutes later, those soaked by the rain were completely dry. As far as thirty miles away, people reported sighting strange light forms in the sky. There were many journalists present who recorded this story, and it filled the newspapers. It was called "the Miracle of the Sun," and it is thought that Mary orchestrated it in order to force the world to believe the predictions she had communicated to the three children.

THE FEAST DAY OF OUR LADY OF FATIMA IS
THE ANNIVERSARY OF THE
FIRST APPARITION, MAY 13.

the NOVENA

Most holy Virgin, who came to Fatima to reveal to the three shepherd children the treasures of graces hidden in the recitation of the rosary, inspire our hearts with a sincere love of this devotion, so that by meditating on the mysteries of our redemption that are recalled in it, we may gather their fruits and obtain the conversion of sinners, the conversion of Russia, and (mention your other requests) *which we ask of you in this novena, for the greater glory of God, for your own honor, and for the good of people. Amen.*

(Recite one Our Father, one Hail Mary, one Glory Be.)

Our Lady of the Rosary of Fatima, pray for us!

**Say this novena nine times in a row
for nine days in a row.**

Our Lady of Perpetual Help

REFUGE IS THE OFFERING MADE TO US by our Lady of Perpetual Help. This icon, painted by a thirteenth-century Greek artist, is one of the most beloved images of Mary and her Son. In it, the child Jesus has just run to his mother in such a fright that one of his sandals is dangling off his feet. Mary calmly shields him, confident in her power to protect him. On either side of them are the objects of the Child's fear. The archangels Gabriel and Michael have revealed to him the cross, the spear, and the sponge, foreshadowing his future torment and execution. Since the birth of her Son, Mary knew he was destined to suffer and die for mankind, yet she firmly believed in his redemption. Therefore, she was able to calm the child Jesus in this moment of anxiety. If God himself can reach out to Mary for refuge, then anyone is able to approach her, no matter what we fear, our future or our past actions. Regardless of how we may judge ourselves, she has total belief and faith in us. It is said that our Lady of Perpetual Help never, ever refuses a request, no matter how small or frivolous it may seem. Many who have felt unworthy to call on her in their direst need report hearing a calm voice saying, "Why don't you just ask?"

An icon is a form of religious imagery employed by the Eastern Orthodox Church. This particular image of our Lady of Perpetual Help is a visual parable; there is no written record that the child Jesus was ever frightened by the two archangels. It does, however, offer a brilliant example of the magnanimity of Mary upon which one may meditate. It is thought that the honor shown to an icon is im-

MATER PERPETUI SUCCURSUS
ORA PRO NOBIS

You are called the refuge and the hope of sinners; be my refuge and be my hope. Help me, for the love of Jesus Christ; stretch forth your hand to a poor, fallen creature.

PRAY TO OUR LADY OF PERPETUAL HELP FOR REFUGE ANYTHING

mediately transmitted to its subject. This is why people pray so fervently as they kneel in front of an icon. This painting of our Lady of Perpetual Help was owned by a wealthy merchant from Crete in the fifteenth century. He eventually brought it to Rome, keeping it in his home, then donating it to the Church of Saint Matthew the Apostle. Many miraculous cures and favors were reported by people who prayed in front of it. This image became very popular, attracting many to venerate it.

When Napoleon sacked Rome in 1789, the Church of Saint Matthew was destroyed. A priest hid the icon to prevent its theft or vandalization. It was forgotten for the next sixty-four years, until the Redemptorist fathers came into possession of the icon. The Pope ordered them to make the dissemination of this image one of the main roles of their order. The Redemptorists distributed reproductions of the picture and talked about it in missions and homilies around the world. By the twentieth century, 1.8 million Spaniards belonged to the Archconfraternity of Our Mother of Perpetual Help, ten thousand shrines and altars were dedicated to her in France, and devotions in her honor were observed in thousands of churches throughout the world. The original icon of our Lady of Perpetual Help can be viewed in the Church of Saint Alphonus in Rome.

THE FEAST DAY OF OUR LADY OF
PERPETUAL HELP IS JUNE 27.

the NOVENA

See at your feet, O Mother of Perpetual Help, a poor sinner who has recourse to you and confides in you.

O Mother of Mercy, have pity on me! You are called the refuge and the hope of sinners; be my refuge and my hope. Help me, for the love of Jesus Christ; stretch forth your hand to a poor, fallen creature. I recommend myself to you, and I want to devote myself to your service forever. I bless and thank almighty God, who in his mercy has given me this confidence in you, which I hold to be a pledge of my eternal salvation.

(Mention your request.)

Mary, help me. Mother of Perpetual Help, never allow me to lose my God.

(Recite the Our Father, Hail Mary, and Glory Be three times each.)

Say this novena nine times in a row for nine days in a row.

Our Lady of Mount Carmel

In this novena, we are offered the protection afforded us from being a member of a family. The more extensive our family, the more safely we are able to walk through the world. Our Lady of Mount Carmel represents the role of Mary as mother of the family of man and honors Mary's protection of the ancient sect of contemplatives who settled Mount Carmel, as well as the symbol of this protection, the scapular. Those who wear this religious picture in present day declare their commitment to Jesus. Devotion to our Lady of Mount Carmel is extremely widespread throughout the world. This novena is particularly effective when we are feeling vulnerable and in need of protection. All are welcome to recite it. In saying this novena, one accepts a role in the extended spiritual family of the Carmelites.

The spiritual legacy of Mount Carmel goes back to 800 B.C., when the prophet Elijah ascended the holy mountain of Carmel in Israel and began a life of contemplation and prayer. In his prophetic visions, Elijah became aware of the coming of the Mother of God. He and his followers mystically dedicated themselves to her, and it was the descendants of the followers of Elijah who were among the first to be baptized by the Apostles. Upon meeting Mary, they were overcome with her majesty and sanctity and they returned to the mountain of Carmel to build the first chapel ever dedicated to the Madonna.

Mount Carmel continued to be a place of pilgrimage and spiritual retreat, housing many hermits who devoted themselves to prayer and contemplation. These hermits

REGINA DECOR CARMELI

© PEKA
4/509
Germany

Behold us, your children. We glory in wearing
your holy habit, which makes us members
of your family of Carmel, through which we
shall have your powerful protection
in life, at death, and even after death.

became the first order of Carmelite friars. During the Crusades, the Saracens began making it difficult for these monks to continue their holy practices. A young English pilgrim, Saint Simon Stock, had joined the group while on a visit to Jerusalem. This ultimately resulted in the order's move to England in the year 1241. The Baron de Grey gave the monks a manor house in the town of Aylesford. In England, the Carmelites developed from a loose-knit group of monks into a traveling society of mendicant friars, opening schools and mission houses in the major capitals of Europe. In 1251, Saint Simon Stock had a vision of Mary in the house in Aylesford. She handed him the first scapular and said, "This shall be the privilege for you and all Carmelites, that anyone dying in this habit shall not suffer eternal fire." This scapular consisted of two brown wool panels joined by strings, to be worn over the shoulders. On one panel was a woven image of Mary holding the baby Jesus. Today, the scapular has this image on one panel and an image of Mary handing the scapular to Saint Simon Stock on the other. The word "scapular" comes from a form of clothing worn over the shoulders as an apron; it is part of the religious habit of monks, nuns, and friars.

Through the years the scapular given to Saint Simon Stock became the symbol of a way of life and an expression of being open to God and his will. It also honors Mary by asking her for her protection, and it establishes a bond between us and the original saints of Mount Carmel.

The feast day of Our Lady of Mount Carmel is July 16.

the
NOVENA

O most holy Mother of Mount Carmel, when asked by a saint to grant privileges to the family of Carmel, you gave assurance of your motherly love and help to those faithful to you and to your Son. Behold us, your children. We glory in wearing your holy habit, which makes us members of your family of Carmel, through which we shall have your powerful protection in life, at death, and even after death. Look down with love, O Gate of Heaven, on all those now in their last agony! Look down graciously, O Virgin, Flower of Carmel, on all those in need of help! Look down mercifully, O Mother of our Savior, on all those who do not know that they are numbered among your children! Look down tenderly, O Queen of All Saints, on the poor souls!

(Pause and mention your request.)

(Recite one Our Father, one Hail Mary, one Glory Be.)

Our Lady of Mount Carmel, pray for us.

**Say this novena nine times in a row
for nine days in a row.**

The Mother of
Sorrows

F EW CAN COMMISERATE WITH THE GRIEF-
stricken as fully as the mother of Jesus Christ. She was
forced not only to witness the torment and ridicule heaped
upon her only child, but to also stand helplessly by as he
died an agonizing death. Many images of Mary depict her
with seven knives in her heart, one for each of the seven
major sorrows endured by the Blessed Mother in her
earthly life. This novena is invoked by those who survive
the death of a loved one and is a request for relief from the
anguish and pain brought on by unrelenting grief. Because
she is also the great mother figure, Mary suffers for us as a
mother suffers from the hurts her own child endures.

The seven sorrows of Mary are:

The prophecy of Simeon. When Mary offered her forty-
day-old child to God in the temple, Simeon the rabbi held
the baby in his arms and foretold to Mary the oppositions
he would arouse in his life with the words: "This child is
destined for the fall and for the rise of many in Israel, and
for a sign that shall be contradicted. And your own soul a
sword shall pierce."

The flight into Egypt. Soon after the birth of Christ, an
angel appeared to Joseph to alert him of King Herod's plan
to murder all the infants in the country, and the Holy
Family fled to Egypt. Mary had to be terrified for her own
child's safety as well as grief-stricken over the fate of the
doomed children left behind.

The three-day loss of Jesus. When Jesus was twelve years old,
he did not return home and his parents could not find him

MATER DOLOROSA

4/102
Western-Germany

*To whom shall I have recourse in my
wants and miseries if not to you, Mother
of Mercy? You have drunk so deeply
of the chalice of your Son, you can
compassionate our sorrows.*

anywhere. After days spent in a frantic search for their son, Joseph and Mary discovered him in the temple, arguing with the elders.

The meeting of Jesus with his cross. As Jesus was being led to his death on Calvary, Mary was among the crowd to watch while her child was beaten, laughed at, and spat upon as he carried the cross he would die on.

The death of Jesus on Calvary. As Jesus hung crucified on the cross, dying, his mother stood beneath it, watching and waiting for his torment to end. Here the prediction of Simeon was realized, her very soul pierced by a sword.

Jesus being taken down from the cross. As Mary and a few devoted followers were given the body of her Son to bury, she said, "All you who pass by this, look and see if there is any sorrow like my sorrow."

The burial of Christ in the tomb. Here the earthly mother said her final goodbye to the physical manifestation of her Son. At this point, there was no sign that Christ would arise, and Mary had to depend solely on her faith.

In order to bear the incredible tragedy in her life, Mary had to take Christ's viewpoint, and have faith that all was for the good of mankind, that through his suffering the rest of the world would be redeemed. When we pray to our Mother of Sorrows, we ask for the solace to be able to accept our own grievous situation.

The feast day of our Mother of Sorrows is September 15.

the NOVENA

Most holy and afflicted Virgin, Queen of Martyrs, you stood beneath the cross, witnessing the agony of your dying Son. Look with a mother's tenderness and pity on me, who kneel before you. I venerate your sorrows and I place my requests with filial confidence in the sanctuary of your wounded heart.

Present them, I beseech you, on my behalf to Jesus Christ, through the merits of his own most sacred passion and death, together with your sufferings at the foot of the cross. Through the united efficacy of both, obtain the granting of my petition. To whom shall I have recourse in my wants and miseries if not to you, Mother of Mercy? You have drunk so deeply of the chalice of your Son, you can compassionate our sorrows.

Holy Mary, your soul was pierced by a sword of sorrow at the sight of the passion of your divine Son. Intercede for me and obtain from Jesus (mention your request) *if it be for his honor and glory and for my good. Amen.*

**Say this novena nine times in a row
for nine days in a row.**

Our Lady of the Miraculous Medal

THE MIRACULOUS MEDAL IS A PHYSICAL manifestation of the gift of grace that exudes eternally from the Virgin Mary. It was originally called the Medal of the Immaculate Conception, but so many miracles were reported by those wearing it that the name was changed. A Miraculous Medal is a common gift for those receiving the sacraments of baptism, communion, or confirmation. The Virgin Mary herself declared that those who wear this medal around their necks will be the recipients of tremendous graces. It is thought that the medal will keep a soul from sinking into iniquity and lead one to a purer life. The Virgin Mary presented the Miraculous Medal to mankind as a gift and a token reminder that she is always ready to offer assistance.

In 1830, one of the few apparitions of Mary to be sanctioned by the church occurred in the Parisian chapel of the Daughters of Charity of Saint Vincent de Paul. In the first of three visions, a novice nun named Catherine Laboure was awakened at 11:30 P.M. by a "shining child" who led her to the chapel, where she found the Blessed Mother. Speaking with her for two hours, the Blessed Mother told Catherine she had a very difficult task ahead of her. Four months later, on November 27, Catherine experienced another vision in the chapel. She saw a three-dimensional tableau of Mary standing on a white globe with dazzling rays of light streaming from her fingers, and she heard a voice say, "These are the symbols of the graces I shed upon those who ask for them." A frame formed around the Blessed Mother, and within it was written in gold letters, "O Mary, con-

*Obtain for us then a deep hatred of sin and
that purity of heart which will attach us
to God alone so that our every thought, word,
and deed may tend to His greater glory.*

ceived without sin, pray for us who have recourse to you." The voice then told her, "Have a medal struck after this model. All who wear it will receive great graces; they should wear it around the neck." The tableau turned and on the reverse side was a large M with a bar through it and a cross over it. Beneath this M were the hearts of Jesus and Mary, one crowned with thorns, the other pierced with a sword. This vision continued to appear to Saint Catherine several more times until September of 1831. Wishing to remain anonymous, she related these events only to her confessor, Monsignor Aladel. He was given permission by the archbishop of Paris to have the medal struck. The first fifteen hundred were issued in June of 1832, and almost instantaneously a wide variety of healings, changes of heart, and miraculous events were reported by those wearing the medal. However, Saint Catherine Laboure herself could not be induced to appear at any of the canonical hearings investigating the apparitions. Eventually this visit by the Virgin Mary was sanctified on the evidence of the miraculous effects of the medals. Saint Catherine Laboure only revealed herself as the recipient of this vision eight months before her death in 1876. This came as quite a surprise, as she was thought by her superiors to be almost apathetic regarding her faith. She was canonized in 1947.

Because the Miraculous Medal commemorates that Mary was conceived without original sin, remaining in this pure state throughout her earthly life, the feast day honoring this vision is the same day as the feast of the Immaculate Conception, December 8.

The feast day of Our Lady of the Miraculous Medal is December 8.

the NOVENA

Immaculate Virgin Mary, Mother of our Lord Jesus Christ and our Mother, penetrated with the most lively confidence in your all-powerful and never-failing intercession, manifested so often through the Miraculous Medal, we your loving and trusting children implore you to obtain for us the graces and favors we ask during this novena, if they be beneficial to our immortal souls, and the souls for which we pray.

(Mention your request.)

You know, Mary, how often our souls have been the sanctuaries of your Son, who hates iniquity. Obtain for us, then, a deep hatred of sin and that purity of heart which will attach us to God alone, so that our every thought, word, and deed may tend to his greater glory.

Obtain for us also a spirit of prayer and self-denial that we may recover by penance what we have lost by sin and at length attain to that blessed abode where you are the Queen of Angels and of People. Amen.

Say this novena nine times in a row
for nine days in a row.

Our Lady of Guadalupe

OUR LADY OF GUADALUPE REPRESENTS one of the most kindly and motherly aspects of Mary. In this novena she is begging us to appeal to her for comfort. Our Lady of Guadalupe should be invoked whenever we need a nonjudgmental force of love in our lives. Just ten years after the Spanish conquest of Mexico, this apparition occurred on the hill where a temple to the Aztec corn and earth goddess, Tonantzin, once stood. The name Tonantzin means "Our Mother," and this is exactly how Mary asks the people of Mexico to perceive her. It seems she did not appear to give warnings or dire predictions to humanity, but rather to show herself as a merciful mother figure, ready to assist in any request. The only visitation of Mary officially recognized by the church on the North American continent, it is an example of how the Madonna changes her image to resemble the race and culture of the people to whom she appears.

On December 9, 1531, a Mexican-Indian peasant named Juan Diego was walking through the countryside of what is now Mexico City. From the top of a hill a beautiful woman called out to him, asking, "Am I not your mother?" She then told him she was Mary, Mother of God, and that she would like a church to be built upon the ground where she stood. She sent him off to Bishop Zumarraga to make this request. The bishop, upon hearing Juan's story, instructed him to obtain a sign to prove that this was truly an apparition of Mary. Juan, returning to the site, found the woman waiting for him. Again she told him that she urgently desired a church to be built to bear

I am a merciful mother to you and to all your people who love me and trust in me and invoke my help. I listen to their lamentations and solace all their sorrows and sufferings.

witness to her love, compassion, help, and protection. She wanted the world to know that she was a merciful mother to all and desired everyone to trust in her and invoke her in times of need. She instructed Juan to gather roses among the nearby rocks for the bishop. Since it was winter, not a season when roses bloomed, he was surprised to find them growing where she told him to look. After gathering the roses in his peasant's cloak, he presented them to Mary, who arranged them; then he took them back to the bishop. As Juan unwrapped his cloak, and the roses fell out, the bishop was stunned. The roses uncovered an elaborate portrait of the Virgin Mary imprinted on the cloak.

This image still exists and is visited by hundreds of thousands of pilgrims each year. A basilica in Mexico City was erected to house it, thereby fulfilling the Virgin's request for a church. This image offers a very different view of Mary: her features are Mexican-Indian, there are rays of light streaming out from her entire body, and the figure is set among the sun, moon, and stars.

Our Lady of Guadalupe is the patron of Mexico, and her feast is honored by the people of that country with an almost political fervor. In keeping with her own requests, all people of the world should feel free to invoke her for help in solving any types of problems, big or small.

THE FEAST DAY OF OUR LADY
OF GUADALUPE IS DECEMBER 12.

the NOVENA

Our Lady of Guadalupe, according to your message in Mexico I venerate you as the Virgin Mother of the true God for whom we live, the Creator of all the world, Maker of heaven and earth. In spirit I kneel before your most holy image which you miraculously imprinted upon the cloak of the Indian Juan Diego, and with the faith of the countless numbers of pilgrims who visit your shrine, I beg you for this favor: (mention your request).

Remember, O immaculate Virgin, the words you spoke to your devout client: "I am a merciful mother to you and to all your people who love me and trust in me and invoke my help. I listen to their lamentations and solace all their sorrows and sufferings." I beg you to be a merciful mother to me, because I sincerely love you and trust in you and invoke your help. I entreat you, our Lady of Guadalupe, to grant my request, if this should be the will of God, in order that I may bear witness to your love, your compassion, your help and protection. Do not forsake me in my needs.

(Recite "Our Lady of Guadalupe, pray for us" and Hail Mary three times.)

Say this novena nine times in a row for nine days in a row.

the Div*t*

The Infant of Prague

Few novenas promise the instantane-
ous results of those to the Infant of Prague. It necessitates
a suspension of all doubt as it is completed in one day over
a nine-hour time span. Perhaps the most invoked aspect of
Christ in the world, this novena promises that anything is
possible for those who believe. Christ is presented as both
a kindly child and a king. The Infant of Prague is a statue
of the child Jesus dressed in actual clothing. Instead of the
modest garments of a poor child, he is wearing the sump-
tuous gown of royalty. Because the Infant of Prague looks
like a little doll, we are welcome to approach him with the
open faith of a child. Reflecting the faith of Jesus, the
novena requires an intensity of devotion. Many people
have a version of this statue in their homes, as it is said to
guarantee abundance. This novena, frequently utilized by
those in financial difficulties, can be said during any desperate situation.

The Divine Child, a nineteen-inch wax sculpture, was
brought to Prague, Czechoslovakia, by a Spanish princess
who had received it from her mother as a wedding gift. She
in turn bequeathed it to her daughter, Princess Polyxena.
On becoming a widow in 1623, Polyxena decided to devote the rest of her life to doing charitable works. The extremely poor order of Carmelite monks of Prague were her
favorite beneficiaries. Bringing the statue, she promised,
"As long as you will venerate this image, you will not lack
anything." The statue of the Divine Child was installed in
the chapel, and the monks became aware of an immediate
change in their material and spiritual fortunes. In 1631 the

Divine Infant of Prague, dearest Jesus, you who so compassionately taught, "If you can believe, all things are possible to him who believes," have pity on me now. I do believe. . . .

Pray to the Infant of Prague for Abundance Epidemics Desperation

monks had to flee their monastery because of an invasion by Sweden. In the ensuing confusion the statue was left behind, only to be thrown on a trash heap by the invading army. Miraculously, it was found seven years later by a priest named Father Cyril, who had been particularly devoted to the Divine Infant. Though it was made of wax, the only damage sustained by the statue was its missing hands. Devotions to the Divine Infant, returned to its altar in the chapel as the once again poverty-stricken Carmelites began to rebuild their monastery, were revived with great fervor. While Father Cyril was praying before the statue, he heard the words: "Have pity on me and I will have pity on you. Give me my hands and I will give you peace." Though money came to the order, it was felt that it should be put to use for more important causes than the repair of a statue. Again Father Cyril heard a voice while in prayer: "Place me near the entrance of the sacristy and you will receive aid." A passing stranger, seeing the broken statue, offered to have it repaired. When the Divine Infant seemed to be responsible for several cures during an epidemic, the priests moved the statue to the main church so that the public could also benefit from its graces. In 1642 Baroness Benigna von Lopkowitz had a beautiful chapel built for the Divine Infant, where it remains to this day. Many make pilgrimages to Prague to see the original little statue that has inspired so many copies around the world.

THE FEAST OF THE INFANT OF PRAGUE IS THE SAME DAY AS THE HOLY NAME OF JESUS, JANUARY 14.

the NOVENA

Divine Infant of Prague, dearest Jesus, you who so lovingly said, "Ask, and it shall be given you; seek, and you shall find; knock, and it shall be opened to you," have mercy on me now, and through the intercession of our most holy Mother, I humbly ask you to grant me the grace I need.

(Mention your request.)

Divine Infant of Prague, dearest Jesus, you who so compassionately taught, "If you can believe, all things are possible to him who believes," have pity on me now. I do believe; help me. Increase my weak faith through the Blessed Mother's intercession; I humbly ask you to answer my request.

(Mention your request.)

Divine Infant of Prague, dearest Jesus, you who once said to the Apostles: "If you have faith even like a mustard seed, you will say to this mulberry tree, 'Be uprooted and be planted in the sea,' and it will obey you," hear my prayer, I humbly ask. Through the intercession of Mary most holy, I feel certain that my prayer will be answered.

(Mention your request.)

Because this novena is said for those in great distress or emergency situations, it is completed in one day. **Say this novena nine times in a row at the same time every hour for nine consecutive hours.**

The Sacred Heart of Jesus

DEVOTIONS TO THE SACRED HEART OF Jesus began in the seventeenth century. Completely changing all perceptions of Christ as an image, Saint Margaret Mary's vision of Jesus with his heart in flames, exposed and surrounded by thorns, became the predominant visual metaphor of his sacrifice and ardent love. Devotions to the Sacred Heart promise to bring peace in the family, blessings on all undertakings, and a refuge at the hour of death. The heart is the seat of love in the body. The wounded heart not only represents what Jesus took on for humanity at the crucifixion, but also his ongoing pain as he watches over the world. Jesus exposes his heart to all of mankind, leaving it in a vulnerable state. He asks all to call on him for favors in a similar state of total trust.

On December 27, 1673, a young Visitation nun in Burgundy, France, named Margaret Mary Alacoque was praying in the convent chapel when she heard a strong inner voice that identified itself as Jesus Christ. Not fully trusting herself to receive a message from Christ, she began to believe in it as this voice spoke to her more clearly. In subsequent visits, Jesus explained to her that he wanted his heart honored in the form of human flesh, as it is represented in the now familiar depiction of the Sacred Heart. Christ also requested a specific devotion for honoring this aspect of his love for mankind. Those who follow the devotion were to attend mass and take communion on the first Friday of each month for nine months in succession. In addition, one hour was to be spent on the Thursday night before the first Friday in meditation on the image of the Sacred

*Sacred Heart of Jesus, I have asked you for
many favors, but I earnestly implore this one.
Take it, place it in your open heart. When
the Eternal Father looks upon it, he will
see it covered with your Precious Blood.*

Pray to the
Sacred Heart of Jesus for
Family Peace Anything

Heart. This was to serve as a reminder of the night Christ spent in the Garden of Gethsemane, as he contemplated his final hours on earth. As she envisioned an image of the Sacred Heart, Saint Margaret Mary heard the words "Behold the heart which has so much loved men that it has spared nothing, even exhausting and consuming itself in testimony of its love. Instead of gratitude I receive from most only indifference, by irreverence and sacrilege and the coldness and scorn that men have for me in the sacrament of love."

A slow and clumsy woman, Saint Margaret Mary was scorned by her mother superior when she informed her of this visitation. She was judged as delusional and barred from carrying out any of the devotions she was instructed to perform. She fell ill and was near death. The mother superior told her that if her health improved, she would take it as a sign that these were truthful revelations. Saint Margaret Mary prayed and recovered within one day. The mother superior kept her word and an understanding confessor, Claude de La Colombière, became a great ally in getting church officials to recognize the importance of the devotion of the Sacred Heart of Jesus. Though Saint Margaret Mary's visions were never officially sanctioned, the sacredness of the devotion was recognized on its own merit. Saint Margaret Mary Alacoque was canonized in 1920.

THE IMAGE OF THE SACRED HEART OF
JESUS IS DISPLAYED IN MANY HOMES
AS IT IS BELIEVED TO BRING
HARMONY TO THE FAMILY.

the NOVENA

NOVENA OF CONFIDENCE
TO THE SACRED HEART OF JESUS

O Lord Jesus Christ, to your most Sacred Heart I confide this intention. Only look upon me, then do what your love inspires. Let your Sacred Heart decide. I count on you. I trust in you. I throw myself on your mercy. Lord Jesus, you will not fail me.

(Mention your request.)

Sacred Heart of Jesus, I trust in you.

Sacred Heart of Jesus, I believe in your love for me.

Sacred Heart of Jesus, your kingdom come.

Sacred Heart of Jesus, I have asked you for many favors, but I earnestly implore this one. Take it, place it in your open heart. When the Eternal Father looks upon it, he will see it covered with your Precious Blood. It will no longer be my prayer, but yours, Jesus. Sacred Heart of Jesus, I place all my trust in you. Let me not be disappointed. Amen.

Say this novena nine times in a row for nine days in a row

The Holy Spirit

THIS IS THE OLDEST NOVENA, DATING BACK to the very birth of the church and its importance cannot be underestimated. When Christ first appeared to the apostles forty days after the crucifixion, he sent them to Jerusalem to await the Holy Spirit and instructed them to pray for nine days. This novena, written in the Middle Ages, is said for nine days prior to Pentecost, the fiftieth day after Easter, and is still the only novena officially prescribed by the Church. Addressed to the Third Person of the Blessed Trinity, it is a powerful plea for the light, strength, love, and wisdom needed by all. In art, the Holy Spirit is always depicted as a white dove.

Each of the nine days was given a different prayer with a different subject to contemplate. After each daily prayer, the Our Father and Hail Mary are to be recited once each and the Glory Be is to be recited seven times. The two prayers on the following pages are to be recited every day of the novena as well.

You are the strength and light of my soul.
In you I live and move and am.
I desire never to grieve you by unfaithfulness
to grace, and I pray with all my heart to be
kept from the smallest sin against you.

the
NOVENA

ACT OF CONSECRATION
TO THE HOLY SPIRIT

On my knees before the great multitude of heavenly witnesses I offer myself, soul and body, to you, Eternal Spirit of God. I adore the brightness of your purity, the unerring keenness of your justice, and the might of your love. You are the strength and light of my soul. In you I live and move and am. I desire never to grieve you by unfaithfulness to grace, and I pray with all my heart to be kept from the smallest sin against you. Mercifully guard my every thought, and grant that I may always watch for your light and listen to your voice and follow Your gracious inspirations. I cling to you and give myself to you and ask you, by your compassion, to watch over me in my weakness. Holding the pierced feet of Jesus and looking at his five wounds, and trusting in his precious blood and adoring his opened side and stricken heart, I implore you, adorable Spirit, helper of my infirmity, so to keep me in your grace that I may never sin against you. Give me grace, O Holy Spirit, Spirit of the Father and the Son, to say to you always and everywhere, "Speak, Lord, for your servant is listening." Amen.

PRAYER FOR THE SEVEN GIFTS
OF THE HOLY SPIRIT

O Lord Jesus Christ, who before ascending into heaven promised to send the Holy Spirit to finish your work in the souls of your apostles and disciples, grant the same Holy Spirit to me that he may perfect in my soul the work of your grace and your love. Grant me the Spirit of Wisdom, that I may despise the perishable things of this world and aspire only after the things that are eternal; the Spirit of Understanding, to enlighten my mind with the light of your divine truth; the Spirit of Counsel, that I may ever choose the surest way of pleasing God and gaining heaven; the Spirit of Fortitude, that I may bear my cross with you and that I may overcome with courage all the obstacles that oppose my salvation; the Spirit of Knowledge, that I may know God and know myself and grow perfect in the science of the saints; the Spirit of Piety, that I may find the service of God sweet and amiable; the Spirit of Fear, that I may be filled with a loving reverence toward God and may dread in any way to displease him. Mark me, dear Lord, with the sign of your true disciples and animate me in all things with your Spirit. Amen.

FIRST DAY: *The Holy Spirit*

> *Holy Spirit! Lord of Light!*
> *From thy clear celestial height,*
> *Thy pure beaming radiance give!*

Almighty and eternal God, who have vouchsafed to regenerate us by water and the Holy Spirit, and have given us forgiveness of all our sins, vouchsafe to send forth from heaven upon us your sevenfold Spirit, the Spirit of Wisdom and Understanding, the Spirit of Counsel and Fortitude, the Spirit of Knowledge and Piety, and fill us with the Spirit of Holy Fear. Amen.

SECOND DAY: *The Gift of Fear*

> *Come, thou Father of the poor!*
> *Come, with treasures which endure!*
> *Come, thou light of all that live!*

Come, O blessed Spirit of Holy Fear, penetrate my inmost heart that I may set you, my Lord and God, before my face forever; help me to shun all things that can offend you, and make me worthy to appear before the pure eyes of your Divine Majesty in heaven, where you live and reign in the unity of the ever Blessed Trinity, God without end. Amen.

THIRD DAY: *The Gift of Piety*

> *Thou, of all consolers best,*
> *Visiting the troubled breast*
> *Dost refreshing peace bestow.*

Come, O Blessed Spirit of Piety, possess my heart; enkindle therein such a love for God that I may find satisfaction only in his service, and for his sake lovingly submit to all legitimate authority. Amen.

FOURTH DAY: *The Gift of Fortitude*

> *Thou in toil art comfort sweet,*
> *Pleasant coolness in the heat;*
> *Solace in the midst of woe.*

Come, O Blessed Spirit of Fortitude, uphold my soul in times of trouble and adversity, sustain my efforts after holiness, strengthen my weaknesses, give me courage against all the assaults of my enemies, that I may never be overcome and separated from you, my God and greatest Good. Amen.

FIFTH DAY: *The Gift of Knowledge*

> *Light immortal! Light divine!*
> *Visit thou these hearts of thine,*
> *And our inmost being fill.*

Come, O Blessed Spirit of Knowledge, and grant that I may perceive the will of the Father; show me the nothingness of earthly things, that I may realize their vanity and use them only for your glory and my own salvation, looking ever beyond them to you, and your eternal rewards. Amen.

SIXTH DAY: *The Gift of Understanding*

> *If thou take thy grace away,*
> *Nothing pure in man will stay,*
> *All his good is turned to ill.*

Come, O Spirit of Understanding, and enlighten our minds, that we may know and believe all the mysteries of salvation, and may merit at last to see the eternal light in your light, and in the light of glory to have a clear vision of you and the Father and the Son. Amen.

SEVENTH DAY: *The Gift of Counsel*

> *Heal our wounds—our strength renew;*
>
> *On our dryness pour thy dew;*
>
> *Wash the stains of guilt away!*

Come, O Spirit of Counsel, help and guide me in all my ways, that I may always do your holy will. Incline my heart to that which is good, turn it away from all that is evil, and direct me by the straight path of your commandments to that goal of eternal life for which I long. Amen.

EIGHTH DAY: *The Gift of Wisdom*

> *Bend the stubborn heart and will;*
>
> *Melt the frozen, warm the chill;*
>
> *Guide the steps that go astray!*

Come, O Spirit of Wisdom, and reveal to my soul the mysteries of heavenly things, their exceeding greatness, power, and beauty. Teach me to love them above and beyond all passing joys and satisfactions of the earth. Help me to attain them and possess them forever. Amen.

NINTH DAY: *The Fruits of the Holy Spirit*

> *Thou, on those who evermore*
>
> *Thee confess and thee adore,*
>
> *In thy sevenfold gifts, descend:*
>
> *Give them comfort when they die;*
>
> *Give them life with thee on high;*
>
> *Give them joy which never ends. Amen.*

Come, O Divine Spirit, fill my heart with your heavenly fruits, your charity, joy, peace, patience, benignity, goodness, faith, mildness, and temperance, that I may never weary in the service of God, but by continued faithful submission to your inspiration, may merit to be united eternally with you in the love of the Father and the Son. Amen.

additional
prayers

Many novena instructions call for other traditional prayers, which are presented here.

THE SIGN OF THE CROSS: (This is said at the opening and closing of each of the prayers below.)

In the name of the Father, and of the Son, and of the Holy Spirit. Amen.

THE LORD'S PRAYER

Our Father, who art in heaven, hallowed be thy name; thy kingdom come; thy will be done on earth as it is in heaven. Give us this day our daily bread; and forgive us our trespasses as we forgive those who trespass against us; and lead us not into temptation, but deliver us from evil. Amen.

HAIL MARY

Hail, Mary, full of grace! The Lord is with you; blessed are you among women, and blessed is the fruit of your womb, Jesus. Holy Mary, Mother of God, pray for us sinners, now and at the hour of our death. Amen.

GLORY BE

Glory be to the Father, to the Son, and to the Holy Spirit, as it was in the beginning, is now, and will be forever. Amen.

topic *index*